Endorsements

We live in uncertain, challenging times. Unexpected cr[...] in, trying to devour us with fear. Cindy Saab has written a Bible study that will restore your hope and give you rock-solid strength. The uniqueness of this book is that there are three levels of participation—and you can choose how deep you're ready to go as you identify your needs, study God's Word, and apply Scripture to your life. This is a study you can do on your own, but better yet with a group of friends. It's life-changing!

Carol Kent, Executive Director of Speak Up Ministries, speaker, and Author of *When I Lay My Isaac Down* (NavPress)

Stuck? Cindy Saab will help you move beyond the pain, beyond the hurt, beyond the storm into the peace and presence of God. This six-week Bible study, *Beyond: Finding Strength and Hope through Unexpected Storms*, will help you move forward.

Pam Farrel, author of 58 books including best-selling *Men Are Like Waffles, Women Are Like Spaghetti*

Cindy has provided a powerful resource to remind us that when the waves crash upon us, we serve a Savior who walked on water. He forever holds out his hand of hope. If you could use some encouragement, do yourself a favor and grab a copy of this amazing study!

Erica Wiggenhorn, national speaker and award-winning author of *An Unexpected Revival: Experiencing God's Goodness through Disappointment and Doubt*

Our perspective determines the trajectory and impact of how we respond when rocked with grief, pain, and suffering. In *Beyond: Finding Strength and Hope through Unexpected Storms*, Cindy Saab delivers biblical encouragement and hope on how we perceive the hard seasons that inevitably come our way. Through this excellent six-week Bible study, Cindy teaches us how to reframe our thinking on grief, suffering, and disappointment through the lens of God's Word and his life-giving grace. If you are in a season of hopelessness, *Beyond: Finding Strength and Hope through Unexpected Storms* was written just for you!

Laura Acuña, author of *Still Becoming: Hope, Help, and Healing for the Diet-Weary Soul*

Life is full of unexpected storms. Cindy Saab, in her new six-week Bible study *Beyond: Finding Strength and Hope through Unexpected Storms*, helps us navigate those difficult times. Through biblical principles and examples, personal stories from her life and the lives of others, and thought-provoking questions, she points us to the one who provides strength and hope when life is overwhelming. This is a resource we all need!

Crickett Keeth, women's ministry director at First Evangelical Church (Memphis) and author of *On Bended Knee* and *Before the Throne*

We all go through storms, but we don't always go through them well. *Beyond: Finding Strength and Hope through Unexpected Storms* is a powerful study, not just because it reveals the strength and hope that God offers to his children during their darkest days, but because it gives real-life testimonies of women who are now "beyond the storm." Having served as Cindy's pastor, I am amazed at how God brought her through some difficult storms. It has been said that God does not waste our suffering. This study is proof of God's goodness to his children even in the midst of great suffering. What a joy to see Cindy not only experience new peace in Christ but comfort others with the same comfort she received from God (2 Corinthians 1:4).

Senior Pastor Tyler Thompson, New England Bible Church, Andover, MA

As someone who has sailed the seas, I know the importance of a place to secure one's boat during rough weather. Having a source of security for the storms of life is the same. Cindy carefully guides her reader, battered by life's troubles, with great sensitivity. Even if you are not facing a storm at the moment, my suggestion is to study this book now and put down anchor. You will have reassurances at hand when you need them to not only survive a storm but to come out the other side with victory.

Rachel Britton, author, speaker, codirector of reNEW
spiritual retreat for writers and speakers

Ladies! This is a must-do Bible study if you are in the midst of a life storm, are still in recovery mode after the storm has passed by, or want to be better prepared for when the next storm hits. Being a New Englander and an admitted beach bum, I love Cindy's usage of the ocean theme throughout the study! In my decades of counseling and coaching, I have helped women navigate the turbulent waters and move forward in life. Cindy sums it up well in week 5 when she says, "We can stay stuck where we are or we can choose to go, to move, to reach out, to follow, to try something new, to go past our comfort zone. There has to be movement on our part." I am praying for you as you journey and am confident you will not regret the investment of time to gain healing and insight through this study.

Dr. Mel Tavares, pastoral care counselor, mental health coach, author, speaker

I know that many women will grow in the Lord through this study. Cindy starts and ends with the Word of God, utilizing the life experiences of Christians to illustrate how his strength sees us through all things. My prayer is that this book, and the conversations it creates, will encourage women to set their hope firmly on the person and work of Jesus Christ.

Matthew Lourdeau, associate pastor of New England Bible Church, Andover, MA

I love this book! Whether you need some top-level "Sea Surface" encouragement, the deepest-level "Ocean Trench" spiritual healing, or anything in between, Cindy Saab's got it for you right here. You'll find helpful acronyms like, STOP: Stand still, Tell God all about it, Observe how God has rescued you, Praise God for being your refuge. Plus there are journaling sections, fill-in-the-blanks, checkboxes, and so much more. No matter your learning style, Cindy's got you covered. Armed with Scripture and hope, you'll emerge from every reading opportunity full of joy and anticipation regardless of your circumstances coming in. Highly recommend!

Marnie Swedberg, international leadership mentor

How I wish I'd had a Bible study like this years ago when I was in the midst of my own devastating personal storm. Whatever your struggle, here you will find help and hope. Cindy Saab gives you a rich treasure of true stories, relevant Scriptures, and practical principles in a powerful resource you can return to with each fresh step you take. You will discover that the three levels of participation to choose from—foundation, application, and reflection—provide you daily with sound biblical truth, wisdom, and encouragement for your weary soul. You will be blessed!

Sandi Banks, author of *Anchors of Hope: Finding Peace Amidst the Storms of Life*

Cindy has written a beautiful Bible study to help comfort anyone that is going through a storm. These are stormy days that we are living in, and everyone could use comfort through Scripture to help with the storms of life. Many times we need tools to help us dive deeper into those Scriptures to bring peace to our minds and hearts through the truth of God's Word. Cindy has written a beautiful guide to do just that. As a counselor, I would recommend this to any clients who have found themselves in a storm of life.

Jennifer Hand, author of *My Yes Is on the Table* and
executive director of Coming Alive Ministries

In recent years, I've experienced a wave of storms cushioned by calm seasons in life. I love Cindy's heart and approach to prepare you, her reader, to face these storms of life, looking way beyond your own strength to keep your head above water. Cindy repeatedly emphasizes in *Beyond* where to find your strength: by diving into God's Word daily! As a joy-seeker myself, I encourage you to pick up this book to weather your storms so that you can be prepared through your happy or hard circumstances for all the Lord promises to you beyond your wildest imagination!

Christine Trimpe, award-winning author, speaker,
joy-seeker, and health & wellness coach

BEYOND

A 6-WEEK BIBLE STUDY

BEYOND

FINDING STRENGTH AND HOPE
THROUGH UNEXPECTED STORMS

CINDY SAAB

Published by Redemption Press, PO Box 427, Enumclaw, WA 98022.
Toll-Free (844) 2REDEEM (273-3336)

Redemption Press is honored to present this title in partnership with the author. The views expressed or implied in this work are those of the author. Redemption Press provides our imprint seal representing design excellence, creative content, and high-quality production.

The author has tried to recreate events, locales, and conversations from memories of them. In order to maintain their anonymity, in some instances the names of individuals, some identifying characteristics, and some details may have been changed, such as physical properties, occupations, and places of residence.

Unless otherwise indicated, all Scripture quotations are from the Holy Bible, New Living Translation, copyright ©1996, 2004, 2015 by Tyndale House Foundation. Used by permission of Tyndale House Publishers, Carol Stream, Illinois 60188. All rights reserved.

Scripture quotations marked (NASB) are from the (NASB®) New American Standard Bible®, Copyright © 1960, 1971, 1977, 1995, 2020 by The Lockman Foundation. Used by permission. All rights reserved. www.lockman.org.

Scripture quotations marked (NIV) are from the Holy Bible, New International Version®, NIV®. Copyright © 1973, 1978, 1984, 2011 by Biblica, Inc.™ Used by permission of Zondervan. All rights reserved worldwide. www.zondervan.com. The "NIV" and "New International Version" are trademarks registered in the United States Patent and Trademark Office by Biblica, Inc.™

Scripture quotations marked (CEV) are from the Contemporary English Version. Copyright © 1991, 1992, 1995 by American Bible Society. Used by Permission.

Scripture quotations marked (ESV) are from The ESV® Bible (The Holy Bible, English Standard Version®), copyright © 2001 by Crossway, a publishing ministry of Good News Publishers. Used by permission. All rights reserved.

Scripture quotations marked (KJV) are from the King James Version, public domain.

Scripture quotations marked (MSG) are from THE MESSAGE, copyright © 1993, 2002, 2018 by Eugene H. Peterson. Used by permission of NavPress, represented by Tyndale House Publishers. All rights reserved.

ISBN 13: 978-1-64645-623-9 (Paperback)
978-1-951310-34-9 (ePub)

Library of Congress Catalog Card Number: 2022951502

In memory of
my mother, Elizabeth Brewster.
Her life exemplified a praying woman
who trusted God for everything,
stood on the promises of God,
spoke the truth of God's Word, and
proclaimed God's love and faithfulness.

Contents

Introduction

I am thrilled that you have grabbed a hold of this study, and I pray deeply it will be a powerful, resourceful tool to carry with you through the various stages of your life storm. Unwanted, unexpected, devastating, and destructive, life storms come in many shapes and sizes and carry different labels, such as addiction, death, infertility, divorce, diagnosis, disappointment. We all have a life-storm story. We all hurt. We all have experienced gut-wrenching pain.

I am so grateful to the many women who have shared their unexpected life-storm stories throughout this study. And to you, reader, let me say how very sorry I am for your storm, trial, devastation, and grief in this season. Keep in mind, this storm is something you are going through. You will not be in this situation forever. Even though we can be a support beam to one another, we desperately need a Savior to carry us through the unforeseen tumultuous waters and dark skies. Truly God alone is our anchor and our only hope. "This hope is a strong and trustworthy anchor for our souls. It leads us through the curtain into God's inner sanctuary" (Hebrews 6:19).

This study consists of lessons I learned along the way, as God brought me not only through but *beyond* the storm. And yes, you can get through the storm if you choose to reach out and seek the God of refuge. Our stories may vary in flavor, but the effects of the storms are the same—devastation. Pain is pain and intense sorrow seeps into the deepest crevices of our soul leaving us heartbroken. Life as we know it is shattered. Our wounds are profound, and we need a healing salve.

My heart's desire is that this study will encourage you to seek the loving, strong arms of God so he can carry you through. Our part is to surrender our weary, shattered heart to God. He will exchange those tears of pain, hurt, and disappointment with warm fresh healing tears. He is our Savior, Redeemer, and Restorer. May this study be a resource that you can refer back to for each fresh step you take. Sometimes we will take a baby step together, and other times we will make a deep dive into the truth of God's Word to find our sure foundation. The God of hope will meet you, and as you take that first faith step, you will discover new strength and peace for each day. A place *Beyond*! That is when we lean fully into our Savior, surrendering all our shattered pieces to the God of hope. He alone will heal the fragmented pieces of your soul and clothe you with overwhelming layers of comfort, peace, love, healing, and trust. At times, he is the only one we can trust, for he is faithful and true.

Getting the Most out of This Study

*B*eyond: *Finding Strength and Hope through Unexpected Storms* is a six-week study with five daily lessons each week. If possible, I encourage you to work on your homework a little every day. That way you can reflect on God's Word and his anchor of hope during the day.

Throughout this study, Scripture is quoted mostly from the New Living Translation (NLT), but other translations are used. When the text and exercises invite you to open the Bible, you may want to use an online Bible resource, like Biblegateway.com or a Bible app, to explore the different translation options.

A unique feature of this study guide is the three levels of participation to choose from: Sea Surface, Challenger Deep, and Ocean Trenches.

Sea Surface

Sea Surface level is the top layer of the ocean, a transitional level that interacts with the wind and waves. It is a transitional level for us as well. As we read stories and words of encouragement, we will work our way through basic questions that don't require a lot of time. My prayer is that each section will serve as a buoy, a guide floating alongside to carry you and ride this wave out with you.

Challenger Deep

Challenger Deep is a watery depth where we experience high water pressure. As we plunge deeper into the Word of God by God's grace and our faith in God, we will venture out and take our next step of faith. Challenger Deep encourages us to seek wisdom and receive understanding by applying Scripture. When applied, these biblical principles promote a shift in your mindset. A change in thought is the soil for a change in action.

Ocean Trenches

Ocean Trenches are deep places where seeping hurts and grief may reside, a place we need to go to examine our hurts and learn to move past them. We will take a moment to pause, silence our heart, soul, and mind, and then creatively pour out our thoughts as journal entries and prayers. We will also ask reflective questions that proclaim a new joy, a new beginning, a new story that is beyond what we could have hoped for—life beyond. When we dig deeper and lay out our thoughts, we learn to reposition and move forward.

The journaling sections offer space to creatively express yourself by writing a prayer, singing a song, or drawing a picture in a way that makes a deeper connection with yourself and God. As I share lessons and stories from others who have walked this road before you, my heart's desire is that this Bible study will serve as a compass to God. The Holy Spirit will come alongside to comfort and guide you, infusing you with strength as you follow him forward and move to the other side of your grief.

Week One

REFUGE
in the Riptides

Grasp that the
God of hope
is your refuge
in your season
of suffering.

Taking Refuge and Finding Freedom

Refuge: Shelter or protection from danger or distress[1]

Have you ever found yourself outdoors when suddenly the sky opened up in a torrential downpour? You take off running, hoping to find a place of refuge that's safe and warm. Did you know that we can be soaked inside as well as outside? Our insides can be soaked in pain. "When we stay soaked in pain, it affects us mentally, emotionally, relationally, and spiritually."[2] John 16:33 tells us, "Here on earth you will have many trials and sorrows." We all arrive at that time and place when we need a refuge, a safe place to reside after we have been hit hard with a life storm and are dealing with unbelievable circumstances.

I felt caught in a riptide of turbulent waters when several family members and friends passed around the same time my marriage of almost three decades ended in divorce. It was a life-altering experience that left me crippled by emotional pain. During those dark days Jesus shined the brightest. He assured me he would always be with me and filled me with his comforting peace.

With a heart of surrender, I gathered the shattered pieces of my life and handed them to the only one trustworthy, my Lord and Savior. God my healer lovingly began to heal each layer of woundedness. When we allow the Lord to heal our deepest wounds, he fills us with immense peace and lifts us to higher joy.

As with any type of loss, grief arrives and is processed in unpredictable waves. You don't receive a grand announcement informing you of your next wave of grief. One day I was at the doctor's office filling out routine paperwork and had to check the box indicating my marital status. I was hit with a wave of shame, sadness, and grief as I told myself, *You are no longer married*. I wanted to run out of the office. I closed my eyes for a moment and asked the Lord to help me. Dr. Michelle Bengtson reminds us that, "He longs to bring help, hope, and healing to those places that have previously brought you only shame."[3] There will always be memories and triggers to remind you of what once was. Acknowledge where you are now, and choose to live victorious today and every day unto the Lord.

Even in the in-between times, when life seems to be smooth sailing, all we have to do is turn on the evening news to hear about bizarre people doing the unimaginable. Yes, we are living in troubling times, but do not forget that we do have shelter from danger and protection from distress. So whether we are seeking refuge from a current life storm or from a worldwide event, we have Jesus! Believing God is your refuge is a basic first step.

David fled from unsafe people who wanted to kill him. Twice, King Saul attempted to kill David by flinging a spear at him (1 Samuel 18:10–12). David fled to a cave as he waited for the disaster to pass. The cave of Adullam (refuge) became David's hiding place. Adullam was a town about 25 miles southwest of Jerusalem. You may not have had someone fling a spear at you, but you may have had many other things that were unfair, a form of betrayal, or simply not right. Have you ever felt like you were not safe and you just wanted to get away from it all? Maybe you wanted to run away and hide. Perhaps you're waiting for the disaster to pass before you come out again.

Sea Surface

David ran into the loving arms of God, because he knew that God was his refuge from dangerous situations and dangerous people. We are told to make God as our refuge. This is done by asking and believing God to be our refuge, our protection.

In 1 Samuel 19, we find several examples of how God provided divine protection over David's life.

Read 1 Samuel 19:1–7. How did God use Jonathan to protect David from King Saul?

_____

_____

Read 1 Samuel 19:11–17. How did God lead Michal to protect David?

_____

_____

While David hid from Saul, he poured out his heart to God. "Have mercy on me, my God, have mercy on me, for in you I take refuge. I will take refuge in the shadow of your wings until the disaster has passed" (Psalm 57:1 NIV).

Why do you think David repeats the phrase, "Have mercy on me?"

_____

_____

David seeks God's protection from the violent storm of destruction. Where does David take refuge?

_____

_____

"He will cover you with his feathers, and under his wings you will find refuge" (Psalm 91:4 NIV). Wings are a beautiful, powerful metaphor for protection and refuge.

Here are some additional wing verses.

- Hide me in the shadow of your wings. (Psalm 17:8 NIV)
- Take refuge in the shadow of your wings. (Psalm 36:7 NIV)
- Under whose wings you have come to take refuge. (Ruth 2:12 NIV)

Challenger Deep

Sometimes I like to read the same Scripture in several translations to get a fuller understanding. Read Psalm 61:4 in various versions.

- NIV: I long to dwell in your tent forever and take refuge in the shelter of your wings.
- NLT: Let me live forever in your sanctuary, safe beneath the shelter of your wings!
- CEV: Let me live with you forever and find protection under your wings.

Draw ✐ a line to match the Scripture verse with the description.

NIV	Safe beneath
NLT	Take refuge
CEV	Find protection

To view additional refuge Scriptures, go to **Appendix A.**

When we take refuge in God, he is our shield and strength. "My salvation and my honor depend on God; he is my mighty rock, my refuge. Trust in him at all times, you people; pour out your hearts to him, for God is our refuge" (Psalm 62:7-8 NIV).

What instruction is listed in verse 8?

_____

_____

David did that very well. He poured out his heart to God and shared every aspect of what was going on in his life. There he met God as his refuge. Will you meet God today as your refuge?

When the storm is raging, we need to S.T.O.P. and pour out our hearts to God. A stop sign can be a divine reminder of how to pour out our hearts to God.

S – *Stand still.* Be honest with yourself and God about what concerns you.

T – *Tell* God all about it—every dreadful, horrifying, frightful detail.

O – *Observe* how God has rescued you (resources, people, guidance, and direction).

P – *Praise* God for being your refuge, your protector, the God of hope.

Ocean Trenches

In Psalm 62, David is encouraged by reflecting on who the Lord is, that the Lord is sufficient and gives rest to all who seek a quietness of heart. God is the source of strength and salvation. Even though David had many reasons to fear, he chose to believe by faith the promises of God. Faith is the antidote to fear and despair.

Psalm 142:2 gives us specific instruction. "I pour out my complaints before him and tell him all my troubles."

What complaint do you need to pour out before him today? Use the space below to tell him about it.

_____

_____

How did you feel as you told God about your storm?

_____

_____

Did you feel any release of tension?

_____

_____

Lifting Burdens and Finding Rest

When was the last time you received an invitation for an upcoming occasion? Was it for a baby shower or wedding? Or maybe it was for a birthday, retirement, or going away party? In my office I have a save-the-date card for an upcoming wedding, and on my calendar, I have a couple of holiday events scheduled, not to mention numerous birthday party invitations from friends and family. Invitations are usually celebratory announcements of distinguished occasions from people who hold special places in our hearts.

Did you know that Jesus also sends us many invitations? Look at Matthew 11:28 (NIV), "Come to me, all you who are weary and burdened, and I will give you rest."

He calls to all who are weary, worn-out, overwhelmed, heavy-hearted, discouraged, and struggling. The one who is carrying the weight of the world on her shoulders and feeling weighed down by her burdens with no relief or hope in sight. A burden is anything that causes you to worry. Many burdens are related to loss, such as death, illness, financial hardships, guilt, traumatic events, and relational stresses. When God bears our burdens, it means we no longer have to.

Sea Surface

Read Matthew 11:28–30 (NIV).

> Come to me, all you who are weary and burdened, and I will give you rest. Take my yoke upon you and learn from me, for I am gentle and humble in heart, and you will find rest for your souls. For my yoke is easy and my burden is light.

Circle the phrase that resonates with you at this very moment.

Come to me	I will give you rest	Burden bearer
Learn from me	I am gentle and lowly in heart	My burden is light
	You will find rest for your soul	

I would circle You will find rest for your soul as I am grieving the loss of my mom, an aunt, and a friend in a two-week span. My heart hurts. Jesus invites us to come to him daily as he is our daily burden bearer.

Match the burden-bearer Scripture reference below with the verses.

Psalm 55:22 (NASB)	Cast your burden upon the Lord and He will sustain you; He will never allow the righteous to be shaken.
Psalm 68:19 (ESV)	Blessed be the Lord, who daily bears us up; God is our salvation. Selah
1 Peter 5:7 (NIV)	Cast all your anxiety on him because he cares for you.

Challenger Deep

Go to **Appendix B: Burden Scriptures**. Refer to this list of verses when you are feeling burdened and need encouragement.

Write out Psalm 68:19 in your favorite version.

_____

_____

Is there something you can give to your daily burden bearer?

_____

_____

We will have sorrows and burdens. Jesus wants us to lift our burdens, sorrows, disappointments, and heartaches to him. He invites us to cast all our cares on his shoulder. Not just the teeny tiny ones, but the ginormous ones too. "In Psalm 68:19, the word 'amas' means to bear a burden. The picture is that of God carrying our burdens for us rather than carrying us directly."[4]

How do the following verses encourage us to respond to our daily burden bearer?

Psalm 68:32 _____	to the Lord
Psalm 68:19 _____	God our Savior
Psalm 68:4 _____	to God and to his name
Psalm 68:26 _____	all you people
Psalm 68:35 _____	be to God

Ocean Trenches

If you're feeling weighed down with the cares of the world, have a heavy heart for your loved ones, and are emotionally and physically exhausted as you process your grief, come to the burden bearer. For me in this season of grief, I find that I need more physical rest. I long for quiet—a quiet room, a quiet mind, a quiet soul.

How do you give your cares to the Lord? One way is to tell him. If you are carrying a burden today, lay it at the feet of Jesus, for he is waiting with outstretched arms. Give him *all* your cares no matter how big or how impossible they may seem.

In 1 Peter 5:7, we're told to cast all our anxiety on him for he cares for us. Cast means to throw something. In Psalm 55:22 (ESV), we read, "Cast your burden on the Lord, and he will sustain you." Moreover, the word translated *anxieties* is used for burden in Psalm 55:22. It means "cares, concerns, things one is anxious or worried about."[5]

Recently, all three waves entered my life at the same time. My fifty-three-year-old brother was diagnosed with esophageal cancer, my mother stepped into a deeper stage of dementia, and I needed emergency surgery—all during the COVID pandemic. Because my brother Paul realized his prognosis was inevitable, unless the Lord intervened, he immediately took a proactive stance to prepare and take care of his family. He closed his business and took care of a few household projects that needed to be done. He was the kind of guy that everyone wanted as their friend. Happy-go-lucky and hard-working, he was a fun friend, considerate brother, caring father, and loving husband to his wife, Sharon. They were adorable together, always teasing and joking with one another. They truly loved being with each other and especially enjoyed cooking together. We always were thrilled when it was their turn to host family dinner, because we knew it would be a delectable meal. I planned ahead to arrive hungry so I wouldn't miss a single morsel of the many courses. Usually, I could make a meal with the appetizer alone, but I saved room for the main meal. And let's not even talk about dessert. This cancer journey was a monumental wave for our family, too colossal for us to navigate. We had to depend on the Lord and trust him to carry us through when our hearts were breaking. Jesus wants us to lift our burdens, sorrows, disappointments, and heartaches to him.

Write a prayer pouring out all your concerns and heartaches. List every single detail of your burden that you are carrying to God today.

Dear heavenly Father,

_____

_____

_____

_____

How do you feel knowing that God is our burden carrier?

_____

_____

Facing Fear and Finding Courage

Have you ever noticed that life doesn't always play out as we had planned? Like when Emma found herself admitted in a sterile, bleak hospital room instead of checking into a fabulous resort for her "girlfriend vacation." Fear abruptly crashed the scene without notice or invitation as she thought of her pain and discomfort, the potential prognosis, how her life might change moving forward, and maybe even death. Yes, we too can relate to how one fear leads to another and then another until we are dealing with a mountain of fear. It is important to nip that fear thought in the bud so it doesn't compound other fears.

What fear are you facing today?

_____

_____

Sea Surface
Read Psalm 46:1–3 (NIV) out loud.

> God is our refuge and strength,
>   an ever-present help in trouble.
> Therefore we will not fear, though the earth give way
>   and the mountains fall into the heart of the sea,
> though its waters roar and foam
>   and the mountains quake with their surging.

Read those verses again slowly. Name two attributes of God that are mentioned in verse 1.
    God is our _____ and _____
    Dave and Laurie were excited to be expecting their second child! At week 15 in the pregnancy, their dreams were shattered when a routine test showed that their unborn daughter, Elizabeth, had Down Syndrome and a significant heart defect. Doctors encouraged abortion, but they decided to trust God. With tears streaming down her face, Laurie

pleaded with God to heal Elizabeth and asked for strength and courage to accept his will and obey him no matter the outcome. God brought them through the most difficult times with the love and support of family, their church, and friends. Specific help came especially when Elizabeth went to heaven at three months old from Laurie's time with her prayer partner, reading books, and the Bible. In a special and tender moment, Laurie was able to meet and share stories with other young mothers who had also lost a child. These brave moms shared their emotions, tears, and even photos of the child they'd lost.

Read Psalm 46:2 (ESV).

> Therefore we will not fear though the earth gives way,
> though the mountains be moved into the heart of the sea.

What does verse 2 tell you *not* to do?

_____

_____

Listed below are five acronyms for FEAR. Check ☑ your favorite FEAR acronym.

- ☐ False Evidence Appearing Real
- ☐ False Expectations Appearing Real
- ☐ Face Everything and Rise
- ☐ Face It Explore It Accept It Rise Above
- ☐ Face Everything and Run

We all experience fear. Fear of the unknown, fear of what could happen, fear of what did happen, fear of what they might say, fear of what they did say, etc. That is probably why there are over 365 Scriptures on the topic. Fear of the unknown evaporates when you focus on the One who is all knowing.

> Fear of the unknown evaporates when you focus on the One who is all knowing.

When was the last time you were afraid?

_____

_____

Challenger Deep

Read Joshua 1:9 in the New Living Translation and fill in the blanks below.

"This is my command—be _____ and _____!
Do not be _____ or _____. For the Lord your God
is _____ you _____ you go."

First Chronicles 22:13 (NIV) tells us, "Be strong and courageous. Do not be afraid or discouraged."

Here are two more verses to look up. What do they say about why we don't need to be afraid or discouraged?

1 Chronicles 28:20 _____

2 Chronicles 32:7–8 _____

We can be strong and courageous women based on God's power through his Word. Look up these four verses and write down the practical steps given for finding the power in God's Word.

- Psalm 1:2

_____

- Deuteronomy 6:7

_____

- Ezra 7:10

_____

- James 1:22

_____

Circle the instruction which is active in your life.

Circle the instruction which challenges you the most.

Write out a goal from your challenge area that will help you be more consistent.

_____

_____

Ocean Trenches

"Be strong and courageous. Do not be afraid or terrified because of them, for the Lord your God goes with you; he will never leave you nor forsake you" (Deuteronomy 31:6 NIV).

"When God has taken us to a new place of His choosing, and we are in the center of His will. He doesn't say 'good luck' and leave us there He gives us the power to do what He has asked us to do."[6]

This was the verse Brianna clung to when she felt orphaned at nineteen years old. When her dad passed suddenly and her mother fell apart, Brianna had to set aside her dreams and ambitions to step up and be the adult. She was angry. The anger combined with her mom's guilt trip, manipulation, and silent treatment to cause deep anxiety. Brianna responded by becoming withdrawn and hanging out with mentally unhealthy people. When Brianna was married a short time later, her mom did not attend the wedding, inflicting more turmoil. Brianna felt numb and built a wall in her mind to separate herself from her mom. Things began to change when she was invited to a neighborhood Christmas breakfast. She began to attend church, Sunday school, and women's Bible studies, where she met kind, loving people. But more importantly, she met her Lord and Savior. Second Corinthians 5:17 told her she was a new creature in Christ, that her old life was gone and a new life had begun. She devoured her Bible and saw a mental health professional. She now knows you cannot break a person who gets their strength from God. Brianna is truly strong and courageous in the Lord.

Write out Deuteronomy 31:6, then post it somewhere you will see it frequently throughout the day. Memorize it and repeat it when your fear and hurt rise up.

Read the Scripture below and notice God's instructions on how we can be strong and courageous.

> Be strong and courageous, for you are the one who will lead these people to possess all the land I swore to their ancestors I would give them. Be strong and very courageous. Be careful to obey all the instructions Moses gave you. Do not deviate from them, turning either to the right or to the left. Then you will be successful in everything you do. *Study this Book of Instruction* continually. *Meditate* on it day and night so you will be sure to obey everything written in it. Only then will you prosper and succeed in all you do. This is my command—be strong and courageous! Do not be afraid or discouraged. For the Lord your God is with you wherever you go. (Joshua 1:6–9 NLT, emphasis mine)

Which of those instructions most resonated with you?

_____

How do you feel when you read those verses?

_____

Read this selection of fear Scriptures.

- I sought the Lord, and he answered me; he delivered me from all my fears. (Psalm 34:4 NIV)
- I am your God. I will strengthen you and help you. (Isaiah 41:10)
- Don't be afraid, for I am with you; Don't be discouraged, for I am your God. (Isaiah 41:10)
- For I, the Lord your God, hold your right hand; it is I who say to you, "Fear not, I am the one who helps you." (Isaiah 41:13 ESV)

Which verse is the most encouraging?

_____

Write it out and post it somewhere you will see it frequently and can read it out loud.

Describe a time when God delivered you from your fears. How did your fearful thoughts change?

_____

_____

Bearing your Losses and Finding Comfort

When you're going through a painful time in your life, it's hard to imagine God will use it somehow and bring good from it. When the Lord took her only daughter, Elizabeth, home at three months old, Laurie's life was shattered. She was confident she would see her little girl again when she got to heaven, but her heart ached to have a daughter after having two sons. God turned her weeping into joy when he blessed her twenty-four years later with two beautiful granddaughters. Caroline and Addison will never replace Elizabeth, but they certainly help fill the void in Laurie's heart. She's grateful to God for his love, compassion, and mercy in giving her two little girls to love on earth while he holds her daughter until she sees her again in heaven.

Sea Surface
"Therefore will not we fear, though the earth be removed, and though the mountains be carried into the midst of the sea." (Psalm 46:2 KJV)

What are some things, places, or people that have been removed or carried away from your life?

_____

_____

I seldom read these verses without thinking of Elisabeth Elliot. She suffered the loss of two husbands. The first, Jim Elliot, was killed by Auca Indians in Ecuador while trying to reach them with the gospel. The second, Addison Leitch, was slowly consumed by cancer. In relating what these experiences were like, she referred to this psalm, saying that in the first shock of death "everything that has seemed most dependable has given way. Mountains are falling, earth is reeling. In such a time it is a profound comfort to know that although all things seem to be shaken, one thing is not: God is not shaken." She added that the thing that is most needful is to do what the psalmist does later, to "be still" and know that God is God. God is God whether we recognize it or not. But it comforts us and infuses strength into our faltering spirits to rest on that truth.[7]

When we cease trying to control the situation, we cease blocking the divine outcome. We often find a new sense of peace and comfort in knowing that God is sovereign over the world and over our lives. We feel the presence of an all-knowing, all-powerful God. We find peace, comfort, and confidence in knowing who God is, reflecting on how God has helped us in the past, and acknowledging God's promise to never leave us.

> When we cease trying to control the situation, we cease blocking the divine outcome.

"When we are anxious, we are not at peace. Anxiety results from feeling out of control. But if we surrender to God, letting Him be in control, we can remain in perfect peace."[8]

Let's look up some verses that tell us who God is. Match the references with the "God is" statements.

Psalm 34:18	God is close to the brokenhearted
1 John 4:7–21	God is love
John 14:6	God is the truth
Psalm 100:5	God is good
Psalm 25:8–10	God is faithful
John 14:27	God is peace
Nehemiah 8:10	God is joy

What "God is" verse means the most to you today?

_____

_____

Listed below are just a few of the many promises of God. Circle the promise that you will hold tightly today.

- You will keep in perfect peace all who trust in you, all whose thoughts are fixed on you. (Isaiah 26:3)

> We find peace, comfort, and confidence in knowing who God is, reflecting on how God has helped us in the past, and acknowledging God's promise to never leave us.

- Do not be afraid or discouraged, for the Lord will personally go ahead of you. He will be with you; he will neither fail you nor abandon you. (Deuteronomy 31:8)

- I have told you this so that you may have peace in me. Here on earth you will have many trials and sorrows. But take heart, because I have overcome the world. (John 16:33)
- I will guide you along the best pathway for your life. I will advise you and watch over you. (Psalm 32:8)
- Come to me, all you who are weary and burdened, and I will give you rest. (Matthew 11:28 NIV)
- "My grace is all you need. My power works best in weakness." So now I am glad to boast about my weaknesses, so that the power of Christ can work through me. (2 Corinthians 12:9)
- Dear brother and sisters, when troubles of any kind come your way, consider it an opportunity for great joy. For you know that when your faith is tested, your endurance has a chance to grow. (James 1:2–3)
- The Lord himself will fight for you. Just stay calm. (Exodus 14:14)

Challenger Deep

Elisabeth Elliot encouraged us to follow the Psalmist in chapter 46 verse 10. "Be still, and know that I am God! I will be honored by every nation. I will be honored throughout the world."

Be still. Turn your focus from striving in your own strength to releasing everything to the all-knowing, all-powerful God. Stop trying to analyze the situations and come up with the perfect plan or remedy. We don't have the answers.

> A surrendering heart is a heart longing to know God.

We were never meant to try to solve the problems of the whole world or our own lives. With a heart of surrender, commit yourself to the Lord and seek his ways in his time. A surrendering heart is a heart longing to know God.

Read and write out the following Scriptures about comfort in your favorite translation. Place a check next to the Scripture verse that comforts you the most.

- Lamentations 3:22–23

_____

_____

_____

- Psalm 34:17–18

_____

_____

_____

- Isaiah 40:27–31

_____
_____
_____

What about these verses encourages you?

_____
_____
_____

Ocean Trenches

Sometimes, when I am unsure of what to do, I try to analyze the situation from every possible angle and make a list of the pros and cons, but I still can't figure it out. I need to stop striving and release it to the Lord. I need to be still.

Pray right now and ask the Lord to show you an area where you need to stop striving and release it God.

- A chaotic life situation
- A person who is dealing with addiction
- A work concern
- A prodigal child
- A burden that is too large to carry
- A health crisis
- Salvation of loved ones

Write out that concern in your own words.

_____
_____
_____
_____

Now say a prayer of surrender to God today! Or write out your prayer below or in a journal.

_____
_____
_____

Releasing Stress and Finding Strength

Julie didn't think it was possible to find strength when all she could see was the midnight darkness without a glimmer of light. A three-in-one foot surgery aggravated a previous lower-back injury, expanded the injury to her upper back and neck, and resulted in pain from head to toe. She had worked her way through nine chiropractors, eight physical therapists, and numerous orthodontists trying to find a doctor who could offer her an accurate diagnosis, effective treatment, or an ounce of hope. You name the type of doctor, and she has seen one. In the end all they could offer was, "Good news, you don't need immediate surgery. Bad news, you have chronic pain." She was desperate for a diagnosis, a treatment, a solution—refuge for her weary body, soul, and mind. Julie is grateful for the slight improvement she sees in her physical life and for what is being developed in her spiritual life as stated in Romans 5:3–5. "Not only so, but we also glory in our sufferings, because we know that suffering produces perseverance; perseverance, character; and character, hope. And hope does not put us to shame, because God's love has been poured out into our hearts through the Holy Spirit, who has been given to us" (NIV). The Lord continues to guide her as she prays and reads her Bible, and he strengthens her to take her next step.

Perhaps you, too, are worn out, worn down, without an ounce of strength to carry on. Your mind is weary, your body is weary, and your soul is weary. During our weary, worn-out seasons, God gives our souls strength for each day. Lucinda Secrest McDowell shares, "I've learned the deepest lessons for living soul strong in the midst of defeat and brokenness. Those times God reached for me in His grace and mercy—lifting me up and setting me on a new path of hope and healing."[9]

How has God given you strength for today's journey?

_____

_____

Sea Surface

Read Exodus 15:2 in the NIV and fill in the blanks.

"The Lord is my _____ and my _____."

What does Psalm 81:1 tell us to do?

_____

Look up the following verses in The Message translation and write down the theme for each verse.

     Psalm 18:32 _____

     Psalm 18:39 _____

     1 Samuel 2:4 _____

     2 Samuel 22:33 _____

     2 Samuel 22:40 _____

Which of the five themes would you choose for your life today?

_____

Match 🖋 the verses on the left with the encouragements on the right.

Psalm 59:16	Show us your strength
Exodus 15:13	Guide them
Psalm 29:11	Guide the feet
Deuteronomy 4:37	By his presence
Judges 6:14	Great strength
Psalm 59:9	Will sing of your strength
1 Samuel 2:9	Lord gives strength to his people
Psalm 28:7	Strength and shield
Psalm 68:28	Go in the strength you have

Challenger Deep

What does 1 Chronicles 16:11 and Psalm 105:4 tell us to do to find strength?

_____

Do you need strength today? Look to the Lord today for his infusion of hope and building of strength. Many times we remain in a season of lack, weariness, and desperation because we look to other things or people instead of looking at the one who can truly give us strength.

Read Isaiah 30:15 and fill in the blanks.

"In _____ and _____ is your strength."

Write out Isaiah 33:2.

_____

_____

_____

When does this verse tell us to seek strength?

_____

Who does God give strength to in Isaiah 40:29?

_____

How do we renew our strength as stated in Isaiah 40:31?

_____

Read Isaiah 45:24. This verse tells us that the Lord alone is our deliverance and strength. Yet we often look to other people or things. Do you recognize a pattern in your life of when you look to others for strength?

Who or what do you usually look to for your strength?

_____

Identify a time when your strength was totally depleted.

_____

Perhaps you can relate to Isaiah 49:4 (NIV). Have you "labored in vain" or "spent [your] strength for nothing at all?"

What questions are asked in Isaiah 50:2?

_____

_____

_____

What are we instructed to do in Luke 10:27?

_____

Read 1 Corinthians 1:25. What is stronger than human strength?

_____

What does Philippians 4:13 tell us we can do through him?

_____

Read Psalm 73:26. God remains the strength _____.

Ocean Trenches

We find strength when we come to God and receive his grace alone. God strengthens us when we are facing temptations. God strengthens us when we are sad and need comfort.

When do you feel your strength being sapped?

_____

_____

Surrender these areas to the Lord and receive the abundant grace of God. Think back through past struggles or your current challenge. Can you find an example of God's strengthening you to keep moving?

_____

_____

_____

Ask God to give you more of those strength moments.

Write out a definition of strength.

_____

_____

_____

Write out a prayer asking God to infuse every area of your life with his strength.

_____

_____

_____

Draw a picture or write a song of what comes to mind when you think of God's strength.

Week Two

HOPE
in the Sea of Despair

Eliminate waves of despair with waves of hope, joy, and peace.

Reaching Out and Finding an Anchor of Hope

Hope: A feeling of expectation, a desire for a certain thing to happen[10]

Mandy felt hopeless while treading through a divorce after more than twenty years of marriage. She lost life as she knew it and her future all in one destructive sweep. To embark upon the healing process, we must acknowledge our losses and give ourselves permission to grieve. We must choose to go through this season of despair, discouragement, and hopelessness. Going through is the only way to the other side. God provided Mandy the supernatural strength when she felt like she could not take her next breath.

Dr. Michelle Bengtson shares in her book *Hope Prevails: Insights from a Doctor's Personal Journey through Depression*, "In those periods of despair, I had to choose to believe God and trust in His promises rather than trust my feelings."[11]

As we come to the God of hope, we reach for the loving hand of our Savior and giver of life. When we let go of the shattered bits of our lives and trust God, we are essentially reaching for the life raft. Those ruptured pieces are fragments of what we once had and what we had hoped for in the future. "We have this hope as an anchor for the soul, firm and secure" (Hebrews 6:19 NIV).

As we lower our hope anchor in Christ, hopelessness may pound us like the wind and waves, but Christ will steady us with hope, joy, and peace. "May the God of hope fill you with all joy and peace as you trust in him, so that you may overflow with hope by the power of the Holy Spirit" (Romans 15:13 NIV).

When we are dealing with a health crisis, we hope for a different diagnosis or a plan of action from our medical team. If a family crisis arises, we hope for relationships that are loving, caring, nurturing, and supportive. If we are hit with a financial crisis, such as a layoff, recession, or unexpected expense, we hope for a way to recover from a financial setback by setting a budget, seeking professional help, cutting back on expenses, or establishing a new

> Hopelessness may pound us like the wind and waves, but Christ will steady us with hope, joy, and peace.

financial skill set. In an emotional crisis, we hope for a sense of calm so we can see clearly and move toward a positive outcome.

Elizabeth's friends, family, and church family cried out to the God of hope while she lay in the intensive care unit. She was scheduled for a minor surgery which turned into a two-month hospital stay after they nicked her esophagus. During this time she was septic and on a ventilator. When she became responsive, she asked the Lord for more time with her family. Just then, a beautiful arrangement of flowers arrived from her church, and it spoke to her of life. As Elizabeth prayed and listened to inspirational music, the prayers, melody, and lyrics washed over her, bringing healing to her body and soul. Elizabeth is grateful for God's mercy, grace, loving-kindness, and healing miracle and proclaims Christ is her healer.

When we enter God's presence with open hands and heart, the Lord suppresses our doubts and fears and comforts us with overflowing joy, deep peace, and abundant hope. Even if our circumstances have not changed, shifting our focus from our crisis to our God of hope will replace our stress, lack of direction, and turmoil with joy and peace that cannot be explained.

Nancy placed her hope in the Lord for her husband to have a personal relationship with God as his Lord and Savior. She set aside time every morning before going to work to read her Bible and pray for her husband's salvation. For three years she continued to pray before her son invited her husband to attend a Christian Leadership Summit. To her amazement, he said yes. That weekend her husband committed his life to Jesus and the Lord worked mightily in both of their lives. Today Nancy and her husband are blessed to attend church and worship the Lord together as a couple.

Sea Surface

Hebrews 6:19 calls hope an anchor for the soul.

Read these different translations and write the words that describe the anchor for the soul.

NIV _____ and _____

ESV _____ and _____

NLT _____ and _____

MSG _____ spiritual lifeline

How have you experienced Christ as your anchor?

_____

_____

In what ways could hope be an anchor in your current storm?

_____

_____

Challenger Deep

Scripture speaks of steadfast hope, that is, choosing to be firm and determined in our belief system. When we stand and position ourselves in that viewpoint, we are steadfast. The word steadfast traces back to the Old English word stedefaest, a combination of stede, meaning "place," and faest, meaning "firmly fixed."

Read each verse.

- Hebrews 10:23
- Hebrews 3:6
- Hebrews 6:11
- Romans 15:4
- 1 Peter 1:13
- Galatians 5:5

Which of these verses is most encouraging to you?

_____

Write your two favorite steadfast hope verses on index cards and memorize them. When you feel the waves of despair crashing over you, repeat these verses to encourage yourself.

Ocean Trenches

Elizabeth and her family went through another storm of losing their home due to loss of a business. When moments of discouragement and disappointment arose, Elizabeth spent time in God's presence and the God of hope infused her with the encouragement, love, care, and strength she needed. Her husband started a new business, and in a few years, they were doing well. Shortly after, God provided an opportunity to purchase a new home that he had been preparing for them all along. Elizabeth and her family held on to God's Word knowing that he would see them through!

When we come to the God of hope, we become strong, we are renewed, we are empowered. "But those who hope in the Lord will renew their strength. They will soar on wings like eagles; they will run and not grow weary, they will walk and not be faint" (Isaiah 40:31 NIV).

Identify four will statements from Isaiah 40:31 and write the action below.

Will _____

Will _____

Will _____

Will _____

Identify two things that will not happen as stated in Isaiah 40:31.

    1. _____

    2. _____

Read Isaiah 40:29. What does God give to the weak?

_____

_____

When we place our hope in God, we chose to believe the promises of God. What are we instructed to do in Psalm 42:5?

_____

_____

What is the common theme in the previous two verses?

_____

_____

Identify an area of your life where you are feeling weary.

_____

_____

Pray to the God of hope to infuse you with strength and power in that area.

Putting and Setting My Hope

At times we get stuck in the muck and the mire. We feel like we cannot move and that life will never change or get any better than this. That is a lie from the pit of hell. You will not be where you are stuck right now forever. Sometimes it is as simple as deciding not to stay where you are stuck. Decide to move, go in a new direction, get a different job, try something new, etc. Your decision, your movement will set off a chain reaction. And even if your situation doesn't change immediately, you will change, and that will set you on a different path. When we are feeling swept away by the storm, hope sounds impossible, but we can practice hope by using the word put.

P – *Practice* hope daily.

U – *Unleash* your determination to hope.

T – *Turn* to God to find hope.

We need to put our PUT on. You may even want to stand and say out loud, "Today, I am going to put my PUT on!" The key to surviving any crisis, new season, or devastation, is hope.

- Hope in God's everlasting love.
- Hope stands on God's promises.
- Hope in God blankets you with peace.
- Hope from God will give you strength for today.

Sea Surface

Read Psalm 119:117. When does the psalmist PUT his hope?

_____

How does he put his hope in the Word?

_____

Meditate on Psalm 119:49 (NIV). "Remember your word to your servant, for you have given me hope." The Word of God provides hope and comfort even in suffering. As we share with others how God has comforted us, that same comfort brings hope to others.

Read the following verses about putting our hope in God's Word. What is the outcome of putting your hope in the Word?

Psalm 119:43 _____.
Psalm 119:74 _____.
Psalm 119:81 _____.

"Commit to the long view as He perfects you day by day. In the end, you will experience gratitude for God's teaching as you see the results of His sanctifying inner work."[12]

Challenger Deep

Read Psalm 119:114 (NIV) and fill in the blanks.

"You are my _____ and my _____; I have put my hope in your word."

Dr. Michelle Bengtson reminds us, "There is always hope in spite of degree of the inner pain you are experiencing."[13]

Teresa learned to put her hope and faith in a knowing God who is always with her, even when she fell on the job. She was out for a year and had to have surgery. Bone-on-bone osteoarthritis in her knee combined with an extremely high body weight meant she could not pass the CPR class and would be terminated. She was devastated, hurt, and angry even though she knew her food addiction had made her physically unable to do her job. The hot daggers of pain inside her knee and lower-back spasms left her close to needing a wheelchair.

Broken in all areas of her life, Teresa became bitter and resentful as her health continued to decline. Her toxic relationship with her mom added to her physical and mental health issues. Knowing her days were numbered, she chose to resign from her job before they could fire her. That July her mom passed away. Teresa asked God to open doors for much-needed emotional and physical healing, including weight loss and knee replacement surgeries. Bariatric surgery helped her lose 200 pounds, which allowed her to get her knee replacement and eventually regain mobility.

Before her knee replacement, Teresa attended a writers retreat where awesome women provided physical support to help her up and down stairs. They also provided spiritual and emotional support when they loved and accepted her as she began another layer of healing.

Where can you identify with Teresa's story?

_____
_____
_____

How can you, like Teresa, place your hope in God to help you in this storm?

_____

_____

_____

Perhaps you sense that this is a time of repositioning. A time to set your hope.

Ocean Trenches

Write out a prayer and ask the Lord for the faith, courage, and strength to follow through.

_____

_____

_____

Read Psalm 78:7 in the NIV. Write out this verse.

_____

_____

_____

Who does the psalmist set his hope in?

_____

Do not forget what?

_____

You are to keep what?

_____

Read Psalm 71:14 NIV. Write out this verse.

_____

_____

_____

When will you have hope?

_____

When will you praise him?

_____

Read Psalm 71:14 in the NASB. When will you praise him?

_____

Carol Tetzlaff reminds us, "Each day you will find an opportunity to unleash the power of praise that guides you through a practice that will eventually become a permanent pattern of daily life. These moments will lead you to align your heart in proper worship."[14]

Waiting in Hope and Finding Daily Strength

If I were to ask for a show of hands for how many people love to wait, I probably could count the responses on one hand, if any. Waiting can be hard when we are waiting for a proper diagnosis or treatment, a relationship to be reconciled, a job to open up in our field, a place to live, or our crisis to somehow subside. Not only do we want the answer now, we want the answer yesterday, and sometimes we want the answer to come before we ask the question. We don't like to wait for answers, wait in line, or wait for anything.

"When waiting seems endless, and our faith is wavering, we need to remember. Recalling the ways the Lord has led, protected, and provided for us is critical. At the front of our minds, we must keep a record of all the times He's come through for us over our lifetime."[15]

Sea Surface

Look up these verses about waiting in your favorite translation and place a star next to any verse that resonates with you.

- Psalm 27:14
- Isaiah 40:31
- Lamentations 3:25
- Micah 7:7
- Romans 12:12
- Colossians 1:11

So how do we wait? Psalm 130:5–6 (ESV) says, "I wait for the Lord, my soul waits, and in his word I hope; my soul waits for the Lord."

Where does he put his hope?

_____

How does he put his hope?

In its discussion of Psalm 130:5–6, the *Bible Knowledge Commentary: An Exposition of the Scriptures* shares, "The psalmist testified that he was patiently waiting for the Lord. He compared his wait to that of a city's watchmen looking for the first rays of dawn, for then they would be relieved of their duties by other guards. He eagerly looked for God's new merciful dealings with the nation."[16]

The psalmist not only waits but waits patiently—trusting, believing, and eagerly looking to God. It can be difficult to wait patiently when you are waiting for provision to arrive or for some level of comfort to come. C. S. Lewis shares in *Mere Christianity*, "I am sure that God keeps no one waiting unless he sees that it is good for him to wait."[17] The psalmist is anticipating that God not only hears but answers. But the best answers come to those who wait for God's timing and God's way. God sees before we show; God hears before we tell; God answers before we know. What we view as a delay for the worst outcome is often an intervention for the best outcome.

> What we view as a delay for the worst outcome is often an intervention for the best outcome.

Challenger Deep

"Answers to prayer have to be on God's schedule, not ours. He hears us pray, and He answers according to His will in His own time."[18]

Are you waiting patiently for God's answer today? "If you are in the waiting room for something you desperately desire, be assured that God is orchestrating your life for his own good purposes."[19]

Not long ago, I believed that God was prompting me to revisit a way-out-of-my-comfort-zone writing and speaking task that came with a way-out-of-my-budget cost. I simply prayed if he provided a good portion of the funds that I would believe that as a confirmation for me to proceed in taking that huge step of faith with many more to follow. A month later the funds arrived unexpectedly for the exact amount needed. I've accepted the challenge, believing that he will also equip me for the assignment. As Jennifer Hand says in her book *My Yes Is on the Table: Moving from Fear to Faith*, he "wants you to go all in with God—because God is all in for you."[20]

Strength grows when we exercise our faith muscle and choose to believe, when we wait in expectation with confidence, believing God for the solution. It is a choice. We waste so much time and effort by relying on other people or hoping that our circumstances will change instead of waiting on God. The more we wait on God, the more our confidence builds. The sooner we resolve to wait on God, the sooner we release our concerns and experience sweet surrender.

Matthew Henry's commentary says, "I wait for the Lord; from him I expect relief and comfort, believing it will come, longing till it does come, but patiently bearing the delay of it, and resolving to look for it from no other hand. My soul doth wait; I wait for him in sincerity, and not in profession only. I am an expectant, and it is for the Lord that my soul waits, for the gifts of his grace and the operations of his power."[21]

From Matthew Henry's commentary, how does he wait?

_____

What does he expect?

_____

What does he believe?

_____

What does he resolve?

_____

I wait for him in _____. I am an _____ and it is _____ that _____, for the gifts of his grace and the operations of his power.

Ocean Trenches
Charles Stanley, in *Waiting on God*, says, "Waiting on God means remaining in your present circumstances until you receive further instructions and His intervention."[22]

Select from the following prompts and write a journal entry.

- About a time that God asked you to wait.
- About a time that you chose your timetable instead of God's time.
- About a time that God unexpectedly answered as only he could.

_____
_____
_____
_____

Shattered Heart to Strong Hope

Kim didn't see it coming as unexpected storms don't announce their intentions. Instead they sweep in and ravage everything in their path.

That's what happened one morning in 2005. She didn't notice what type of storm was brewing as she drove to work. It wasn't until she turned around to retrieve something she'd forgotten that she saw dark plumes of smoke had filled the sky as fire consumed her home. A tsunami of emotions swept over her as she pulled into the driveway, soon realizing her youngest daughter and her daddy were still inside. Kim dropped to her knees begging God to find her daughter. The firefighters did.

Hours later, Kim walked the hospital halls and prayed. She cried to the One who saves, choosing to trust him no matter the outcome. Then, moments later, she sat in front of the doctor and faced every parent's worst nightmare. Kim's daughter had died.

Some storms last mere minutes, while others hover and wreak additional havoc. Grief is like that lingering kind. For years after her daughter died, she lived in a haze, struggling to figure out life after the storm. She searched for hope, longed for healing, and prayed. A lot. Kim asked God to reveal himself, demanded, really. She wanted to see his plan, his goodness, and his mercy, especially in such sorrow.

Slowly, he answered her broken heart's cry. Healing came as the Lord tenderly brought comfort and peace through the revelation of the Word. Kim found journaling a helpful tool to process her grief. She also discovered the power in praying through her sorrow, grief, and wells of pain. Ever so slowly, God, through his spirit, bound the wounds fire seared into her heart while leaving the ugliest, most beautiful scar to remind Kim of his goodness in her darkest storm. Scars are a beauty mark of strength.

At times we can feel like our shattered life is beyond repair and restoration. Our only hopeful step is to pick up the pulverized pieces and place them in the loving hands of our Savior so he can repurpose, repair, and rebuild. He makes our lives into beautiful works of art, similar to Kintsugi, the Japanese art of repairing broken pottery with lacquer dusted or mixed with powdered gold, silver, or platinum. We are then stronger than we knew possible for we have a newfound strength. God has infused us with a strong hope because we chose to believe and trust in him.

Sea Surface

> And after you have suffered a little while, the God of all grace, who has called you to his eternal glory in Christ, will himself restore, confirm, strengthen, and establish you. (1 Peter 5:10 ESV)

What four things will Christ do for us?

1. _____
2. _____
3. _____
4. _____

The first step of faith is reminding ourselves that God has been faithful in the past and he does not change, so he will be faithful again. That truth gives us hope that he will provide an outcome better than we are able to imagine.

Walls and Anders tell us in their commentary on 1 and 2 Peter that "This is <u>more than a hope</u>; it is an assertion of <u>what God will do</u>. God will restore or repair whatever is damaged, so the believer will be able to face up to whatever lies ahead. Failure in the past does not doom a person to failure in the future. God will make followers of Christ strong or stable, providing us with courage to go on. He will make us firm and steadfast, so that our foundation in him is secure."[23]

Look, believe, and claim where God wants to restore, confirm, strengthen, or establish you. God brings restoration where we didn't even know we needed. He confirms who we are because of who God is. God infuses and establishes us with his strength.

Check ☑ the boxes that apply to you today.

- ☐ Yes, I believe God himself will restore, confirm, strengthen, or establish me.
- ☐ Yes, God has brought restoration into my life.
- ☐ Yes, God has restored, confirmed, strengthened, or established me.

Challenger Deep

When God brings healing restoration to things that you have lost through suffering and pain, God establishes you with a holy boldness and repositions you with a new placement. God infuses you with his power and strength.

> God himself will perfect your deficiencies, make you ready in every sense. Restoration either in this present life or later—the *God of all grace* will *restore* them or "make them fully prepared and complete" with respect to any resource or

ability which they have lost through this suffering. He will *establish* them firmly in any position, rightful privilege, or responsibility which this suffering has taken from them. He will *strengthen* them for any weakness they have been made to suffer, any inadequacy for overcoming evil which they may have known.[24]

God has identified what he will do. Now let's identify what we can and will do.

- Identify areas in your life where you need to be restored.
- Acknowledge and receive support from God.
- Lean on and exchange your weakness for God's strength.

"Peter offers his audience a final word of comfort. He reminds them that God will empower and ultimately glorify those who remain steadfast in their faith under the weight of their present suffering."[25]

How has God showered his grace upon you?

_____

_____

How has God given you hope?

_____

_____

How has God restored your mind?

_____

_____

How has God strengthened you?

_____

_____

Ocean Trenches

"God is still moving forward with your healing. He is more committed to your wholeness than you are. Transformation can't be rushed."[26]

Write God a thank-you letter for how he has brought you hope, comfort, or restoration.

_____

_____

_____

_____

Fulfilling Hope

Linda could not believe that Karen, her coworker and friend, would take credit for Linda's creative project idea at the quarterly corporate planning meeting. When Linda went home and shared the incident with her husband, his response was less than sympathetic. It was more like, "Who cares what she said." This disappointment added a layer to the numerous times she had been disappointed by friends, family, and even herself. She was overwhelmed as her mountain of disappointment continued to grow in height and width. Linda sensed that she needed to take her focus off her disappointments, so she went to the Lord in prayer. She could have continued to build upon the mountain of disappointment, but she chose to release the work situation to the Lord and continually lay it at the feet of Jesus. Linda felt such peace, even though she had no idea of the outcome. Not too long after, Linda was offered a position for a new division that was opening up. She believed that God had shown her favor because of her obedience. Linda could have continued down the road of disappointment, but that usually leads to other detours, like blaming, shaming, or wearing our disappointments as a cape of shame.

Sea Surface
"Hope does not put us to shame, because God's love has been poured into our hearts through the Holy Spirit who has been given to us" Romans 5:5 (ESV).

According to this verse, what does hope not do?

_____

Let us read a couple of Scripture verses that state the importance of trusting in him.
"They trusted in you and were never disgraced" (Psalm 22:5).
"Anyone who trusts in him will never be disgraced" (Romans 9:33).

When we trust in him, we will never be _____.

Challenger Deep

We also need to realize that everything we hope and pray for does not happen this side of heaven or even at all.

> Some things we hope for in life do not come to pass. When that happens, disappointment sets in. Disappointment produces discouragement; discouragement, unproven character; unproven character, despair. Paul says that we are the recipients of God's love for us, and hope that is based on God's love does not disappoint. Why? God has poured out his love into our hearts by the Holy Spirit, whom he has given us. In Romans 8:16: The Spirit himself testifies with our spirit that we are God's children. No child who is loved by their father has any doubt that the father is trustworthy; any doubt that the hope directed toward the father will not one day be a "tree of life." And the Spirit tells us—in our heart—that we are children of God. A hope which fails of realization does put one to shame, but the hope which is based on the promise of God is assured of fulfilment (cf. 8:24–25).[27]

The immeasurable love of God has been poured out into our hearts. *The Bible Reader's Companion* describes it this way: "God's inexhaustible supply of love is poured out generously by the Holy Spirit who lives within us. Whatever happens to us, we are surrounded by love."[28]

Ocean Trenches

Our hope is found in God's divine abundant love. It is not a question of how much we love God, but a demonstration of God's love for us. God's love overflows without any restraint or limits. God's love is poured in so that hope can be poured out.

Our hope is found in God's divine abundant love. It is not a question of how much we love God, but a demonstration of God's love for us. God's love overflows without any restraint or limits.

How has God poured out and demonstrated his love toward you?

_____

_____

How does God continue to pour out his love within our hearts?

_____

_____

Week Three

TRUST
in the Tidal Wave

To receive freedom
and restoration,
surrender your
broken trust
and unlock your heart.

Bringing Our Broken Trust

Trust: assured reliance on some person or thing; a confident dependence on the character, ability, strength, or truth of someone or something; a person or thing in which confidence is placed.[29]

A tidal wave is "an unusually high sea wave that sometimes follows earthquake."[30] There are three types of ocean waves: wind-driven waves, tidal waves, and tsunamis. Often when we are going through a life crisis, it can feel like we are being consumed by a high sea wave that was triggered by a life earthquake. A tidal wave can also represent a surging of our emotions, when we feel overwhelmed or unprepared to cope with what is happening in life. This is common when one thing happens after another and the waves won't stop knocking us down.

"If we are to trust God, we must learn to see that He is continuously at work in every aspect and every moment of our lives."[31]

Isabella had a bad reaction to medication that caused her heart to race and breathing to become difficult. For months she lived in great fear and anxiety. She got checked out by a doctor and prayed but continued to struggle. Eventually she had to decide if she was going to live in fear or faith. Isabella reflected on her relationship with the Lord and asked herself if she was going to try to solve the problem herself or rely on God. She listened to the Abide biblical meditation app and prayed, but she still stayed up most nights and was unable to sleep. She felt out of control. She confided in a Christian friend who said that what Isabella was going through was not unusual for people who are sensitive to medication. Her friend gave her suggestions on how to cope with anxiety by taking brisk walks, listening to music, and praying. Her friend reminded Isabella that God was with her even in the difficult times. She began a reading plan to read through the Bible in a year, and slowly Isabella started to feel better a little at a time. If he loved her enough to die on the cross to save her from her sins and give her eternal life, surely he loved her enough to take care of the everyday problems. She realized she needed to trust and rely on Jesus. When nothing else really helped, he was there to calm the storm. He knows what is best and perfect for her situation and provides the peace she longs for.

"We honor God by choosing to trust Him when we don't understand what He is doing or why He has allowed some adverse circumstance to occur."[32]

"Let me hear of your unfailing love each morning, for I am trusting you. Show me where to walk, for I give myself to you" (Psalm 143:8).

Sea Surface

We live in a broken world with broken people, an ideal recipe for unbelievable and horrific scenarios. Brokenness can lead to betrayal while wholeness can lead to growth. A profound betrayal from a friend or family member will wound us deeply. Not only is our heart broken but our trust is broken. Broken trust is usually caused by someone we should have been able to depend upon, someone trusted with our whole heart.

What is a broken-trust moment you had (or someone you know)? How did you feel?

_____

Along with our mountain of grief we have a mountain of questions. Now what? What do we do with our broken trust? Can it be fixed? Can we trust again? Will we always walk with a limp to remind us of our injury?

You may be asking yourself, "Should I trust someone who has broken my trust?" The answer is yes and no. If the person who broke your trust is truly sorry for the pain that they have caused you may choose to trust them again. However, if the person is not interested in any type of restoration, does not respect you, is not interested in what you say and feel, or does not want to set any type of boundaries, you may want to reconsider extending your trust. Of course, this is a decision that should be deeply prayed through. Yes, we should offer forgiveness, but seek the Lord's direction on extending trust to that person who so deeply broke your heart by breaking the bond of trust. God is the only one we can fully trust in all matters.

Read Psalm 28:7. Who can you trust with all your heart?

_____

When we trust God, what happens to our hearts?

_____

How did the people in these verses trust God?
    Daniel 6:23 _____
    Daniel 3:17 _____
    Ruth 2:12 _____

Challenger Deep

Read Exodus 15:13 and write down what God will do.

You will _____

You will _____

What is the outcome of trusting God as stated in the following verses?

Isaiah 26:3–4 _____

Psalm 32:10 _____

Proverbs 29:25 _____

Psalm 91:1–4 _____

Psalm 34:4 _____

Ocean Trenches

Psalm 147:3 tells us, "He heals the brokenhearted and bandages their wounds."

Write out a prayer surrendering your broken trust.

_____

_____

_____

_____

Match ✎ the following Scripture verses on the left with God's promises on the right.

Psalm 34:18	I will heal them
Isaiah 57:19	I restore the crushed spirit
Isaiah 57:15	The Lord, who heals them
Isaiah 57:18	I will heal them. I will comfort them

Share a testimony of when you were healed, revived, guided, or restored by God or when your crushed spirit was lifted.

_____

_____

_____

_____

Broken Trust to a Sovereign God

When a relationship has been bruised by broken trust, we question if we should extend trust to that person again, and we find that we may now have trust issues with other people. At times we may also find ourselves asking, "Can I really trust God?"

Sea Surface

How has your broken trust impacted other relationships?

_____

How has your broken trust impacted your relationship with God?

_____

In *Trusting God*, Jerry Bridges wrote, "I desire to encourage God's people by demonstrating from Scripture that God is in control of their lives, that He does indeed love them, and that He works out all circumstances of their lives for their ultimate good. God's people are not immune from such pain. In fact, it often seems as if theirs is more severe, more frequent, more unexplainable, and more deeply felt than that of the unbeliever. Where is God in all of this? Can you really trust God when adversity strikes and fills your life with pain? Does He indeed come to the rescue of those who seek Him?"[33]

Challenger Deep

God, in his love, always wills what is best for us. In his wisdom, he always knows what is best, and in his sovereignty, he has the power to bring it about. John Piper tells us this in *Suffering and the Sovereignty of God*.

> The evil and suffering in this world are greater than any of us can comprehend. But evil and suffering are not ultimate, God is. He does according to his will among the host of heaven and among the inhabitants of the earth, and none can stay his hand or say to him, 'What have you done' (Daniel 4:35). [He declares]

the end from the beginning and from ancient times things not yet done, saying, "My counsel shall stand, and I will accomplish all my purpose" (Isaiah 46:10). Many are the plans in the mind of a man, but it is the purpose of the Lord that will stand. (Proverbs 19:21, 16:9). Therefore, if God is for us, who can be against us? . . . Who shall separate us from the love of Christ? Shall tribulation, or distress, or persecution, or famine, or nakedness, or danger, or sword? God moves in a mysterious way, His wonders to perform. He plants His footsteps in the sea, and rides upon the storm.[34]

Bob and Nancy dove into trusting God when Bob received a diagnosis of stage 3 esophageal cancer on April 1. They soon realized that it was not a joke but their new reality. Nancy sat paralyzed, terrified at the thought of life without her Bobby. Bob retired and Nancy took over managing the house, running their business, and caring for Bob, which didn't leave much time for Nancy.

Then they experienced a business crisis which forced Nancy to retrieve all paper copies of invoices, bills, etc. and reenter an entire year of transactions into the business software so she could do the taxes. Shortly after, Nancy received a new diagnosis of bipolar disorder. Keeping all those life-plates revolving was just too much. She was never meant to carry it all. The Lord intervened and provided a week-long stay in a hospital to adjust her medication and start the therapy she needed then and ongoing. The Lord graciously provided loving friends and family to mow the lawn, send food and beautiful cards, and walk with Bob and Nancy during the endless doctor appointments, hospital stays, and radiation treatments. The power of prayer was evident as Bob had a sense of peace through it all, and they knew that the Lord carried them through.

Maybe you're just starting or are trapped in the middle of a storm. Maybe you have more than one storm colliding. Write one sentence to describe your storm. What does it look like where you are?

_____

_____

Initially storms make us feel weak and powerless, but when God infuses us with courage and power, we come out of the storm a different person. After the storm we have a holy boldness, a holy courage, because we know who we belong to and who will hold us and guide us through life with his truth and light.

Ocean Trenches

Fight to believe the truth, for the truth will set you free. Jesus said, "I am the way, the truth, and the life" (John 14:6) and "he will guide you into all truth" (John 16:13). Combat lies with the truth of God's Word. Here is what John 8:44 tells us about our enemy, Satan. "He has always hated the truth, because there is no truth in him. When he lies, it is consistent with his character; for he is a liar and the father of lies."

We need to identify anything that does not line up with the truth of God's Word and name it for what it is: a lie. Then we replace the lie with the transformational truth of God's Word. We can stand on the promises of God's truth.

When you struggle through the storm, how do these items play out in your life?

Pain _____

Silence _____

Secrets _____

Memories _____

Lies _____

Insecurities _____

Thoughts _____

Write out your struggle and bring it to the Lord in prayer.

_____

_____

What lies are you believing that have your mind imprisoned? Identify the thoughts.

_____

_____

What steps can you take, what truth can you declare, what promise can you stand on today to help you break free of those lies?

_____

_____

Ask your prayer or accountability partner to pray with you and check on you later. If you don't have a prayer or accountability partner, talk to a leader at your church about finding one.

Why We Can Trust God

April 27 is my brother Paul's birthday, and we wanted to do something to express our love for him. We thought, if he had enough strength, he could look out of the living room bay window, and we could drive by singing happy birthday, shouting I love you, and holding posters and balloons. But at the time he was not up for it, as he did not want us to see him in his current state. Finally in May, his wife, Sharon, arranged for his siblings to come round to the back porch and sit six feet apart. So my sister Linda and her husband Mark, myself, and my other brother Frank went to our seats on the back porch. Sharon went in the house to bring Paul out to the porch. Even though I was thrilled that we were going to be able to see Paul in person after such a long time, I had to keep my composure as he stepped out onto the porch. I was taken back with how much weight he had lost and how different he looked. He was no longer the tall, muscular man I remembered. We always joked that, even though he was the baby of the family, he was the tallest of all five siblings. Laughter cut the air as we began sharing childhood stories. "Hey, Paul, do you remember when you used to 'borrow' Linda's car and go for a joy ride before you were old enough to get your license?" The next couple of hours were glorious as we continued to roar with laughter on our trip down memory lane.

Then his medication wore off and it was time for us to leave. We went from much laughter and joyful tears to a deadly silence and tears of sorrow. At that moment we all realized this would most likely be the last time we saw Paul this side of heaven. Paul asked me to pray. I bowed my head, not knowing if I could utter a word. God gave me the strength to share a couple of sentences, and with tear-stained faces, we said our *goodbyes* and *I love yous*.

Jerry Bridges, in his book *Trusting God*, asked a couple of questions that my family and I asked during that time. Maybe you have too.

Did I really believe that a God who loved me and knew what was best for me was in control of my situation? Could I trust Him even if I didn't understand?

Trusting God is worked out in an arena that has no boundaries. We do not know the extent, the duration, or the frequency of the painful, adverse

71

circumstances in which we must frequently trust God. We are always coping with the unknown.

In order to trust God, we must always view our adverse circumstances through the eyes of faith, not of sense.

The faith to trust God in adversity comes through the Word of God alone. It is only in the Scriptures that we find an adequate view of God's relationship to and involvement in our painful circumstances. It is only from the Scriptures, applied to our hearts by the Holy Spirit, that we receive the grace to trust God in adversity.

Can you trust God?

Is he dependable in times of adversity?[35]

Sea Surface

Take a step of faith today and choose to trust God.

Believe what God says about himself, because God does not change.

Write a prayer below telling God in what area you are choosing to trust him. If you don't feel like trusting him, ask God to help you to trust him anyway.

_____

_____

_____

Challenger Deep

Read the verses below and match ✐ them with the statements about trusting God.

Trust in God's power and strength	Psalm 18:2–3
Trust in God's unfailing love	Psalm 13:5
Trust in God's salvation	Isaiah 12:2
Trust nurtured by God's revealed truth	Proverbs 22:19–21
Expressions of trust in God	Psalm 4:5

Which of these powerful verses most encouraged you to trust God more?

_____

Write out Psalm 18:2–3.

_____

_____

_____

_____

Objects can be helpful reminders. I have a couple of rocks in my office. One has the word *Strength* painted in gold lettering. Another rock has Romans 15:13, one of my favorite verses, written on it.

"The various terms used describe God as an object of the most implicit and reliable trust. Rock—literally, 'a cleft rock,' for concealment. Strength—a firm, immovable rock. Horn of my salvation—The horn, as the means of attack or defense of some of the strongest animals, is a frequent emblem of power or strength efficiently exercised (compare De 33:17; Luke 1:69). Tower—literally, 'high place,' beyond reach of danger."[36]

Read Psalm 48:1, Psalm 96:4, and Psalm 145:3. What is the common theme?

_____

Ocean Trenches

Here are a few reasons why we can trust God.

- God is truth. "Make them holy by your truth; teach them your word, which is truth" (John 17:17).
- God never changes. "Jesus Christ is the same yesterday, today, and forever" (Hebrews 13:8).
- God promises to hold us. "Fear not, for I am with you; be not dismayed, for I am your God; I will strengthen you, I will help you, I will uphold you with my righteous right hand" (Isaiah 41:10 ESV).
- God is faithful. "And God is faithful" (1 Corinthians 10:13).

Which of these statements about trusting God are you holding on to today and why?

_____

Which statement are you struggling with today?

_____

Write out a prayer with your struggle and praise.

_____

_____

_____

_____

You Can Trust God Because He Knows

Do you ever feel like no one knows, nor do they care, what you're going through? I think we all have, but it's not true. Don't believe the lie that others don't care. Sometimes they simply cannot relate or may not know what to do to be helpful.

In *Can You Still Trust God? What Happens When You Choose to Believe*, Charles Stanley shares, "Not only did God know about that need, but He knows His provision for meeting that need. Just as your need is no surprise and no mystery to Him, neither is the provision for solving your problem or meeting your need hidden from His understanding or ability. And best of all, God has already prepared for you all that you will need for every day of the rest of your life."[37]

In October 2019, when Paul was diagnosed with cancer, he chose not to mention it to my mother, who was already struggling with dementia. As we gathered at my house during the holidays, my mom turned to Paul and said, "Paul are you all right? You don't look well." Can I just say, a mother knows.

About a month before my brother's diagnosis, my mother, who was living in a lovely assisted-living facility, decided to take a walk and wandered across the street. From that point on, we had to provide overnight care. Some nights we had paid care, but most nights my sister or I slept (not really) in the recliner in her room. As her memory issues became more frequent, we had to make different housing arrangements. So my sister and I took turns having our mother stay with us so we could care for her and spoil her rotten. And then COVID hit. That spring was a hard season for my family as we cared for our mother and dealt with my brother's sickness. My brother passed away in July.

I was in total denial that my brother would pass. Perhaps, it was the only way that I could cope with everything. We explained to my mother that Paul was sick and that the Lord took him home so that he would not be in pain anymore. She kept on saying, "I know, I know. I don't know why everyone is telling me that Paul passed." We believe she was thinking of my brother Michael who passed away over thirty years ago. So there we were, sitting on the front row, in front of the casket, at the funeral home. My mother turned to me and said, "It is amazing. That young man right there could be Paul's twin. At that moment, I calmly said, "Yes, Mom, I know." But inside I had an eruption of emotion so traumatic that the pressure tore my eye. After the funeral I went to the eye doctor to have emergency surgery. During this time God gave us what we needed for each day as we walked out this difficult season. We relied on God for his strength, grace, and mercy to carry us. Even though it was an arduous time, we also sensed God's presence, peacefulness, love, and tender care.

Sometimes all we see is the impossible. We feel like we missed our opportunity or we don't have what it takes, or our tank is empty. Maybe we feel like we're too much of a mess, too young, too old, too tired. The list goes on. Today, choose to believe that God can and that God will.

Sea Surface

We can trust God when:

- We are going through a difficult time
- We don't understand what is happening
- We feel like we do not have options
- We can't believe this is happening to us
- A longing is unfulfilled
- We don't have the provisions we need

Do you need direction and guidance? Read Proverbs 3:5–6.
Do you need hope? Go to Romans 15:13.
Are you longing for peace? Meditate on Philippians 4:6–7.

What will you believe God for today? Be specific.

_____

"And God will generously provide all you need. Then you will always have everything you need and plenty left over to share with others" (2 Corinthians 9:8).

Challenger Deep

As you pray, write out your *praise*,
release your concern,
choose to *trust* your sovereign God,
surrender your heart,
and *ask* the Lord for his answer and his time.

_____

_____

_____

Ocean Trenches

Linda Evans Shepherd shares in her book *Prayers for Every Need* a few guidelines she has gleaned from her prayer life that may help you.

1. You can approach God, even about small matters.
2. God loves you and listens because he wants to have a personal relationship with you.
3. You cannot control God. God will answer your prayers in his time and in his way.
4. The more you bring your requests to God, the closer your relationship will become.
5. The more God answers your little prayer requests, the more you will understand that he really does care for you.
6. As you see God answer your little prayer requests, you will find it easier to trust him with your bigger prayer requests.
7. The more you trust God, the more faith you will have that he will answer you.
8. The more faith you have, the more miracles you will have the ability to see.[38]

I'd like to challenge you to ask God to meet your needs for thirty days. Each day, choose one Prayer Starter word from the list below, and watch God work! If certain words on this list are particularly meaningful to you, use them more than once. If you have a need that isn't on the list, feel free to create your own list.

Prayer Starter: Lord, I pray for . . .

Peace	Abundance	Despair	Grief	Joy
Strength	Wisdom	Courage	Burdens	Calling
Plan	Sorrow	Attitude	New Beginning	Believe
Choices	Purpose	Blessing	Cares	Family
Comfort	Discouragement	Refuge	Endurance	Faith
Fears	Confidence	Healing	Rest	Lead
Doubt	Help	Decisions	Knowledge	Restoration
Hope	Mind/Thoughts	Instructions	Desires	Discipline

I recommend focusing on a specific attribute of God's personality when you pray. Below is a selection of words to choose from, but you may add others to the list as well.

Pray To: Lord, I pray to you as my . . .

Savior	Advocate	Counselor	Mighty God	Lord
Anointed One	Heavenly Father	Awesome	Faithful	Shepherd
Teacher	Promise giver	Rock	Keeper	Deliverer

Linda Evans Shepherd continues in *Prayers for Every Need,* "When life sends us trouble, we should pray. When we experience blessings, we should pray. When a friend or loved one is going through a difficult time, we should pray."[39]

Dear Lord, help us to become women who pray!

Trusting God and Moving On to New Beginnings

While traveling through an unexpected season you eventually come to a crossroad, a place of decision. What will you decide? If you choose to stay where you are, you will sink deeper into the muck, imprisoned by the fallout from your circumstances, believing the lies that your life has evaporated into thin air and that you don't have a choice. If you choose to take a step of faith with a mighty God, you can stomp out the lies and move beyond your past. You will live in the truth of God's Word, stand on the promises of who God says you are, and rely on the character of God. This is a defining moment when you can surrender your past, present, and future and step into freedom with strength you did not know you had.

Trust God as you transition from what you had and who you were into something entirely new. God will amaze you with his faithfulness as he guides you through your desert, your season of grief, to a fresh start with opportunities and experiences you did not know were possible. Only God . . .

Sea Surface

"For I am about to do something new. See, I have already begun! Do you not see it? I will make a pathway through the wilderness. I will create rivers in the dry wasteland" (Isaiah 43:19).

I am not saying we should ignore what has happened. No, we need to acknowledge our losses, but we do not have to stay there. Our unexpected season is not our permanent address. We want to move on.

So let's write out a journal entry about the rough waters you have trudged through this last year.

Challenger Deep

God is making a way in the wilderness and will make a way for you in a mighty miraculous way as only he can.

- There the Lord will be our Mighty One. It will be like a place of broad rivers and streams. (Isaiah 33:21 NIV)
- Mightier than the thunder of the great waters, mightier than the breakers of the sea—the Lord on high is mighty. (Psalm 93:4 NIV)

What hardship or unexpected season are you facing today that God is mightier than?

What we once considered crushing and life altering, in time and by God's grace, becomes a pivotal point to a new direction, a new mindset, a new confidence, new strength.

> What we once considered crushing and life altering, in time and by God's grace, becomes a pivotal point to a new direction, a new mindset, a new confidence, new strength.

And we will discover many new blessings that God has in store for us. "See, the former things have taken place, and new things I declare; before they spring into being I announce them to you" (Isaiah 42:9 NIV).

Prepare your heart and mind to be still so that you can hear God speak to you. God has an announcement for you. Listening for the stillness of God is peaceful and most powerful.

Trust God with all your thoughts.

Trust God with all your hurts.

Trust God with all your what ifs.

Trust God with all your but . . .

How do you prepare your mind to be still?

How do you prepare your heart to be still?

Try these helpful tips for meeting with God daily.

- Find a comfortable, quiet environment where there are not a lot of distractions.
- Be consistent with the time and meeting place.
- Praise God for who he is.
- Praise God for his promises.

- Listen to what God is saying and obey.

Linda Evans Shepherd shares a few things that do not work: "Your life will not change overnight, but as you trust God—one minute, one hour, one day at a time—you will soon discover that he has led you out of this dark place and has provided you with hope and a future."[40]

Ocean Trenches

"You can't make promises to God with strings attached, you can't trade favors with God, and you can't bribe God with a payoff. Don't even think about it."[41]

Select three questions from the list.

What are some obstacles that you face when preparing to hear from God?

_____

Write out or say a prayer to remove that obstacle.

_____

_____

Write a journal entry to record times in your life when it was easier to hear from God.

_____

_____

When is it harder for you to hear from God?

_____

What delays you from obeying God?

_____

_____

How has God helped you through your turbulent waters, your season of loss?

_____

_____

Week Four

LOVE
in Immeasurable Depth

Receive God's ocean
of love washing
over your wounded heart,
proclaiming that you
are valued treasure.

Unloved Heart Rooted and Established in God's Love

Susan shook her head in shock and disbelief. She couldn't comprehend the crushing words from her husband of fourteen years as he announced that he never loved her and it was time for him to live his own life. She stood motionless, unable to process her thoughts. "I am leaving you and I never loved you," played on a loop in her mind. God reminded Susan how much he loved her and valued her. A couple years later she met and married a widower who cherished her. Even though people may change their love status for you, nothing can change God's love for you. God's love is eternal and unconditional. God is love, and he delights in displaying an overflowing fountain of love for us especially when you feel unloved or unlovable.

"Don't allow the disappointment of yesterday to rob you of the hope of today."[42]

Sheila Walsh has this to say. "If you find yourself right now in a place where you are heartbroken, I want to remind you that Christ is very close to the broken-hearted. Our culture throws broken things away, but our Savior never does. He gently gathers all the pieces, and with his love and in his time, he puts us back together."[43]

Charles F. Stanley, from In Touch Ministries, shares, "The Father's love has nothing to do with our merit; it is based solely on his grace, the Son's work of redemption on our behalf, and our secure position in Christ."[44] God pursues us with his immeasurably abundant love, which overflows eternally!

As we discover the ocean of God's love, truth will dispel myths and lies that have held us captive far too long. God's seal of love will affirm our spiritual blessings in Christ and proclaim to us and the world that we are his most valuable treasure.

Paul prayed in Ephesians 3:16–17 (NIV), "that out of his glorious riches he may strengthen you with power through his Spirit in your inner being, so that Christ may dwell in your hearts through faith. And I pray that you, being rooted and established in love."

Sea Surface

Anyone else need to be strengthened by the power of God? During COVID, Joanna felt very alone when she was told she had a cancerous mass on her breast. Joanna and Jeff spent an hour praying in the hospital parking lot before going home to call their adult children. A couple of days later, their children quickly went into support mode, faithfully sending prayers, Scripture, and songs of great encouragement.

Their daughter Jan ordered 200 T-shirts that read "No One Fights Alone" on the front and "#Joanna" on the back. The khaki shirts were printed with black lettering representing being part of an army. Jan shared, "You have an army of people praying for you and every army needs to be uniformed."

Joanna was encouraged to see visible reminders of the army of people praying for her and her family. At church they found whole families wearing their fashionable Joanna army T-shirts. Her brother sent Joanna a photo of his family wearing the T-shirts. A friend shared a photo of wearing the T-shirt while tending to their garden. As they wore the T-shirts, Joanna was reminded that she was loved by family, friends, and God. We are strengthened by the power of God's divine love dwelling in our hearts. "My Father will love them, and we will come and make our home with each of them" (John 14:23).

As Christ inhabits deeper places in our hearts, we experience God's love at deeper levels. Thank God for his divine love and ask him for a deeper dwelling of his presence and his love.

God desires a deeper relationship with each of us. As the apostle Paul puts it, "Let the word of Christ dwell in you richly, teaching and admonishing one another in all wisdom, singing psalms and hymns and spiritual songs, with thankfulness in your hearts to God" (Colossians 3:16 ESV).

Here are some helpful suggestions in preparing for the Word of Christ to dwell in you.

- Read your favorite Bible version slowly.
- Notice any key words or phrases that speak to your heart. You may also want to record the word and phrases in your journal.
- Pray and ask the Lord to speak more deeply to you in what he is teaching you.

Challenger Deep

When we are deeply rooted in Christ, we can accomplish what God has called us to do. When we are rooted in God's love and understand how much he truly loves us, we have a peace and a confident assurance knowing who we are. As we make time to dwell in Christ and walk continually by faith, we become stronger in our relationship with God and live in hope.

"And now, just as you accepted Christ Jesus as your Lord, you must continue to follow him. Let your roots grow down into him, and let your lives be built on him. Then your faith will grow strong in the truth you were taught, and you will overflow with thankfulness" (Colossians 2:6–7).

Our roots need to be planted deeply in the soil of God's love so that we are nourished and become strong in the Lord. Our roots must continually go deeper and deeper into the love of Christ. "Love must become the dominant quality of life, the roots of your existence, the foundation on which all else rests. Such love in your life comes from the divine love."[45] To establish our roots in Jesus means we are dependent on God for everything. He is our sure and true foundation. When we are rooted in Christ, we have a strong faith and rely solely on him for everything.

Just like a tree, we grow into maturity and bear fruit. Jesus provides everything we need to grow and bear the fruit. One way to grow strong roots is to read, study, and meditate on God's Word. I find it helpful to write out Scripture on an index card or a sticky note. I carry it around with me and read it repetitively throughout the day.

How can we develop stronger roots in our life today?

_____

_____

How would you describe being rooted in Christ?

_____

_____

Ocean Trenches

God's love is also the ground upon which a building is constructed. "Love is to be the soil in which their life is to be rooted; love is to be the foundation on which their life is built."[46]

Prior to constructing a building, a soils test determines if the ground can support the weight of the finished building. You want to confirm that you are constructing your home on a buildable lot. A firm foundation is the structure on which you build. If you do not go deep enough in your foundation, you cannot build high.

The love of God needs to be the presiding characteristic in our lives. A storm will reveal the strength of the roots and the foundation in our lives. The strength and courage we find are developed during life's unexpected storms making our soul and strength grow to new heights.

Let's identify and share some ways we can develop a stronger root system and enhance deeper spiritual growth.

Mentor: How can a mentor be beneficial?

_____

_____

Prayer Partner: How can a prayer partner be beneficial?

_____

_____

Spiritual or Life Coach: How can a spiritual or life coach be beneficial?

_____

_____

Let's share why building community with others is important. How does participating in women's Bible study promote growth?

_____

_____

How does participating in a mom's group promote growth?

_____

_____

How does participating in a prayer group promote growth?

_____

_____

Give examples of being in community or receiving fellowship on a regular basis.

_____

_____

Comprehend the Immeasurable Depth of God's Love

May you have the power to understand, as all God's people should, how wide, how long, how high, and how deep his love is. (Ephesians 3:18)

When life is spinning out of control and I need to remind myself of God's love, I immediately go to one of my favorite places in the world, the beach. Even before I get out of my car, I usually roll down my car window so I can get a whiff of the salty air. I love to plant my beach chair at the shoreline so I can get an up-front view of the waves crashing, offering a fine spray mist and the sound of the water slapping the sand. The ocean paints a picture of God's love as I gaze at the horizon, broader than the width of east to west. I can only imagine the depth to the ocean trenches. And to my delight, quite often there is a beautiful sunset reaching to the heavens, displaying a splash of glorious color from the Creator himself.

Sea Surface

Joanna was showered in love from many people who provided support as they knew how. They gave what they could. Joanna's daughter-in-law Sam, a hairdresser, shaved Joanna's head in the privacy of their home. To Joanna's amazement her hair has grown back a different texture and a different color. Shanna went with Joanna to try on wigs. Kathryn sent Joanna eyebrow pencils and suggested she start practicing drawing her eyebrows. Joanna's sister sent her peppermint essential oil to help with the nausea. Joanna also filled a huge box with special notes, song lyrics, prayers, and words of encouragement sent by friends and family. She is so grateful for the overflowing love that was poured out to her and her family.

Name something that reminds you of God's love.

_____

Here are a few Scriptures to reflect upon to remind you of God's love. Place a star next to the Scripture that means the most to you today.

- When you go through deep waters, I will be with you. (Isaiah 43:2)
- God causes everything to work together for the good of those who love God. (Romans 8:28)
- So do not fear, for I am with you; do not be dismayed, for I am your God. I will strengthen you and help you; I will uphold you with my righteous right hand. (Isaiah 41:10 NIV)

Here are a few promises of God's goodness and love. Place a star next to the promise that means the most to you today.

- The Lord is good to all; he has compassion on all he has made. (Psalm 145:9 NIV)
- Give thanks to the Lord, for he is good; his love endures forever. (1 Chronicles 16:34 NIV)
- For the Lord is good and his love endures forever; his faithfulness continues through all generations. (Psalm 100:5 NIV)

Challenger Deep

As we hold on to God's promises, we feel strong in the Lord. There is a sense of security as we know that God's promises are true and cannot fail. We have hope that we can hold on to God's promises as he is faithful and true. We are learning to trust God and we step out in faith believing God. God's promises are provided for us for the taking; therefore, our part is to take that faith step by believing, holding on to, and standing on that promise.

Here are a few statements from other sources. Let's read what they have to say on this topic.

"By faith we lay hold of God's promises. Paul especially wants them to lay hold of God's immeasurable love, a love that fills all things."[47]

"May you experience the love of Christ, though it is too great to understand fully. Then you will be made complete with all the fullness of life and power that comes from God" (Ephesians 3:19).

"As we grow, get settled and grounded, so does our understanding and comprehension of God's love."[48]

"The content of this comprehension is to know experientially the love of Christ that supersedes all knowledge."[49]

"Those who receive grace for grace from Christ's fulness may be said to be *filled with the fulness of God*, according to their capacity, all which is in order to their arriving at the highest degree of the knowledge and enjoyment of God, and an entire conformity to him."[50]

Give examples of what we do not want to be filled with.

_____

_____

What is something that you want to be filled with?

_____

_____

Write out the following verse in your journal, on an index card, or on a sticky note to read daily.

> And I have filled him with the spirit of God, in wisdom, and in understanding, and in knowledge, and in all manner of workmanship. (Exodus 31:3 KJV)

Ocean Trenches

Choose to be filled and not to settle for an empty life. "An empty life is disappointing and dangerous; if the Spirit of God does not fill us, then the spirit of disobedience goes to work and we fall into sin."[51]

Search deep in the crevices of your heart and identify if there is an area in your life that you feel empty.

_____

_____

Is there an area in your life that you feel you are settling?

_____

_____

Write it out, say it out, pray it out, cast it out. Bring it before your heavenly Father who loves you so.

Infinitely more, Immeasurably More

Now all glory to God, who is able, through his mighty power at work within us, to accomplish infinitely more than we might ask or think. Glory to him in the church and in Christ Jesus through all generations forever and ever! Amen. (Ephesians 3:20–21)

Even though at times we have experienced unexpected storms and some with immense loss, we also have been blessed with many unexpected blessings from God both small and immeasurably more. We've had the opportunity to bless others by giving a meaningful gift on a special occasion. And we have been a recipient of an immeasurable gift leaving us speechless with a heartful of gratitude.

Sea Surface

Let's read Ephesians 3:20 in a few different translations.

- ESV: Now to him who is able to do far more abundantly than all we ask or think, according to the power at work within us.
- KJV: Now unto him that is able to do exceeding abundantly above all that we ask or think, according to the power that worketh in us.
- NIV: Now to him who is able to do immeasurably more than all we ask or imagine, according to his power that is at work within us.
- NASB: Now to Him who is able to do far more abundantly beyond all that we ask or think, according to the power that works within us.
- NLT: Now all glory to God, who is able, through his mighty power at work within us, to accomplish infinitely more than we might ask or think.

Sometimes I think I pray too small. If God is able to do immeasurably more, exceedingly abundantly above, then I need to broaden the scope and depth of my prayers.

Would you say you pray in a nearsighted or farsighted fashion? _____

Give some examples of both small and big answered prayers.

_____

_____

Have you asked something *big* from God recently? Have you thought of or hoped for something beyond your wildest imagination?

_____

_____

What would be something that you would ask God for that would take you out of your comfort zone?

_____

_____

Millie experienced her own perfect storm when grief and finances collided. Millie lost her husband at only forty-three years old. She was left feeling frightened, alone, and a little angry. Even though her twin girls were nineteen years old and her son eighteen, she knew it was now her sole responsibility to keep a roof over their heads. She was exhausted from the stress of being a caretaker to her family and felt empty. She also didn't know how she was going to support her family, since she had not been in the workforce for twenty years. She was grateful that her girls and her son all worked for the same company and, during her husband's illness, were allowed to leave at a moment's notice when emergencies came up. But Millie's situation was also known to a sovereign God. Soon after her husband's passing, the vice president of that company was instrumental in getting Millie an interview and job even though she had no current experience. God was faithful and Millie saw that God was with her, protecting her and her family. God opened doors and gave her the strength to pick up and carry on. Millie is now a follower of Jesus Christ and can never thank him enough for being with her during her darkest moments and colliding storms.

Challenger Deep

How would you finish the following sentences:

- God, I know you are able to _____.
- God, I thank you for your faithfulness in the past, and now I thank you for _____.

Ask him for something that only God can do. Think big. Think God.

God I am asking you for _____.

Ocean Trenches

Write about a time when you prayed small and God blessed you abundantly and immeasurably more.

_____

_____

_____

_____

Love of God, Praise to God—a Doxology

The last verse in Ephesians 3 is a doxology. "Glory to him in the church and in Christ Jesus through all generations forever and ever! Amen" (Ephesians 3:21). Merriam-Webster defines *doxology* as "a usually liturgical expression of praise to God. An oral expression of praise and glorification. The word ultimately derives from the Greek verb *dokein*, meaning "to seem" or "to seem good.""[52] Our hearts should continually praise God through every kind of day. Even on those days that we feel we are surrounded by fear or are standing on the front lines, praise turns to protection. Praise God, worship God, to the glory of his name!

According to the *Lexham Context Commentary*, the well-known doxology "Praise God from Whom All Blessings Flow" is "a recognition of God's ability and power that begins with a recognition of God's ability to provide more than is needed. He continues by stating how this is accomplished: it is through God's power that these prayers are answered. The doxology is concluded with a statement of praise directed toward God and this praise is due to God for all generations eternally."[53]

We can express our praise to God with a shout of joy, or a whisper of thanks, by playing an instrumental song or singing meaningful lyrics with hands raised or humbly lowered.

Initially Cheryl reacted with fear, anxiety, and great uncertainty over her breast-cancer diagnosis. She immediately asked for prayer and was anointed with oil by a prayer leader in her church. Cheryl felt God leading her each step of the way to top physicians with the best treatment plan possible. She felt some relief when a dear friend said, "it will go against every natural human feeling and tendency to worry, to fear over this, but begin praising the Lord."

Her granddaughter, Devin gave her this Scripture verse in 2 Thessalonians 3:16, "Now may the Lord of peace himself give you his peace at all times and in every situation." Cheryl claimed this verse over and over again through each procedure along this journey. She continued to praise God, and he used his Word to bring great comfort as each day she faced new challenges. She had never felt such unwavering peace before or after that experience. She was fully healed and continues to praise the Lord!

Sea Surface

Quite often doxologies were expressed at the conclusion of hymns and prayers. As you say or write out your next prayer, close by including one of the doxology Scripture verses from 1 Chronicles 29:10–13.

_____

_____

_____

Challenger Deep

Psalm 29:2 (NIV) reads, "Ascribe to the Lord the glory due his name; worship the Lord in the splendor of his holiness."

We can intentionally express our adoration toward the almighty God throughout the day, beginning by praising God the moment we awaken. We offer our praise as a gift of adoration to him.

"Give unto the Lord your own selves, in the first place, and then your services. Give unto the Lord glory and strength; acknowledge his glory and strength, and give praise to him as a God of infinite majesty and irresistible power; and whatever glory or strength he has by his providence entrusted you with offer it to him, to be used for his honor, in his service."[54]

Even when you feel like everything has been taken from you, you are still able to give to the Lord.

What do you sense the Lord is asking you to praise him for today?

_____

Doxologies are not always at the conclusion of a hymn or prayer. Doxologies are also opening lines of praise, salutations, or opening thanksgiving. They are praise specifically to God the Father, on behalf of Christ, or magnifying the Lamb of God.

Listed below are several doxology Scriptures. Identify words that are repeated in these verses. You may also want to observe if they are an opening or closing doxology, a hymn, praise, thanksgiving, or some other type of verse.

"All glory to God forever and ever" (Galatians 1:5).

_____

"All glory to the only wise God, through Jesus Christ, forever. Amen" (Romans 16:27).

_____

"Blessings on the King who comes in the name of the Lord!" (Luke 19:38).

_____

"Praise God for the Son of David! Blessings on the one who comes in the name of the Lord! Praise God in highest heaven!" (Matthew 21:9).

_____

Ocean Trenches

When do you find it difficult to praise and thank God?

_____

Write out one of the doxology Scriptures from above on an index card. You may want to recite this verse first thing in the morning until you have it memorized. You will be amazed at how your perspective will change when you change your focus to the Most High God.

Never-Ending Love of God

God has given us the ultimate gift of love—salvation. "This is how God showed his love among us: He sent his one and only Son into the world that we might live through him. This is love: not that we loved God, but that he loved us and sent his Son as an atoning sacrifice for our sins. Dear friends, since God so loved us, we also ought to love one another" (1 John 4:9–11).

Clarice's husband David was one of kindest people she ever knew. When he proposed marriage, he added, "Let me be clear about one thing, after God, I am *wife*-focused." For the fifteen years they were married, he kept his word, always putting her needs above his.

When David died of complications from acute myeloid leukemia, Clarice found herself widowed for the second time in twenty-three years. Though she felt many of the same emotions—sorrow, loneliness, pain, and confusion—this time she knew God was in control.

Clarice shared, "I was decades older in my faith walk and more mature. Years of studying God's Word had strengthened my foundation. Knowing David was with the Lord and no longer suffering was huge—and still is."

Having previously experienced the death of a spouse, Clarice knew better than to try to rush the grief process. She wanted her grief to honor David's memory and took these specific and practical steps:

- Didn't hold back tears but sat before the Lord and mourned
- Combatted "brain fog" by writing lists
- Accomplished a few mundane tasks each day
- Enjoyed memories of their time together
- Didn't pretend everything was okay but let family and friends love and help her
- Spent time with God and in his Word daily, and
- Took it easy on herself . . . as she knew David would

Clarice says, "One of the verses that reaffirms my hope is 2 Corinthians 5:1, 'For we know that when this earthly tent we live in is taken down (that is, when we die and leave this earthly body), we will have a house in heaven, an eternal body made for us by God himself and not by human hands.'"

Sea Surface

"A new command I give you: Love one another. As I have loved you, so you must love one another" (John 13:34 NIV). This verse commands us to love one another.

In a moment we will take a closer look at "one another" verses in the Bible, but first we are going to view what God said about how *not* to treat one another.

Match 🖎 the references on the left with what not to do on the right.

Colossians 3:9	Not become conceited, provoking, and envying
James 4:11	Do not slander
James 5:9	Do not lie to one another
Galatians 5:15	Do not grumble against each other
Galatians 5:26	Stop passing judgement on one another
Romans 14:13	Devour/destroy each other

Challenger Deep

If I asked if you have ever experienced what not to do from another person, you would likely say yes to almost all of them. Honestly, if I asked if you inflicted another person with what not to do, you might have the same answer. Yes. We live in a fallen world, and we are all sinners. There are consequences for sins.

Circle a "what not to do" that was done to you.

Think about it for a moment and then go before your loving heavenly Father and give your concern, consequences, anger, bitterness, etc. to God. Seek to live in freedom and not carry that burden any longer. Pray for yourself and pray for the individuals involved. Thank the Lord!

Circle a "what not to do" that you have done to another.

Think about it for a moment and then go before your loving heavenly Father and confess your wrongdoing. Pray for any anger, bitterness, or justification for the wrongdoing, and lay it at the feet of Jesus. Pray for yourself and pray for the individuals involved. Thank the Lord!

Ocean Trenches

Now we will look at the "one another" verses reference tool. The "one another" verses are listed in **Appendix C**. These verses tell us what we should be striving for. We love God by loving others well. Here are a couple of ways that you may want to challenge yourself.

- Write out a "one another" verse daily in your journal and follow with a time of prayer and reflective journaling.
- Tewnty-Five-Day Challenge: Read, write, and pray a "one another" verse for the next twenty-five days.
- Weekly Challenge: Read, write, and pray a "one another" verse on a weekly basis.

JOY
Minded in the Grains of Grief

Scattering your
grains of grief
cultivates a
life of contentment
and a life of true joy.

Discovering Joy, Desiring God brings Him Glory
"Joy: a source or cause of great happiness"[55]

Throughout the *Beyond* Bible study we have named diverse life storms and identified a myriad of losses. For us to continue to ride out this storm, we need to acknowledge the only way out is through. We need to make a decision. We can stay stuck where we are or we can choose to go, to move, to reach out, to follow, to try something new, to go past our comfort zone. There has to be movement on our part.

As we float along in obedient trust with Jesus, we are amazed that one day, somehow, we once again begin to feel something beyond that excruciating pain. Slowly, we notice the pain is not as intense. And then it happens—we feel a flicker of joy. The joy cultivates, expands, and even flourishes. There has been a shift. Instead of every dreadful moment focused on the storm, our gaze is laser focused on God and what he is doing. It's true. For a time, we are counting our losses, and then one day, we have a joy we never knew possible. A joy unspeakable. "We can choose to remain frustrated during times of waiting or we can look for the hidden joys and blessings of the moment."[56]

Take a moment and realize just how far you have come. What changes or adjustments have you made?

_____

_____

Let's look for the joy.

Gail knew all too well the insurmountable, numbing pain associated with losing a child. For days she did not know if Aaron, her college-age son, was alive or dead as they searched the river where a group of students went rafting. Gail was heartbroken beyond repair. She felt drained and lifeless. Nothing going on around her mattered. At first, she was able to hold on to the hope we have in Christ and then vacillated between hope, anger, and disbelief. She couldn't pray, sing, or go to church. She began to see the situation through the eyes of Christ. God's Word kept her from losing herself in the muck and mire of grief.

Although she still feels the pain of missing Aaron every day, she tries to help others who have asked for help. For herself, other people offered assistance, but she didn't want to hear it. She only wanted to hear what God said and not rehash or compare stories with other people. God constantly showed himself to her in ways only God could. Gail felt like it was her job to stay focused on him, even when things got tough. She held on to the hand of God and his promises and found joy through her grief journey.

Sea Surface

Are you joyful today? To be truthful, I have sometimes confused being happy with being joyful. I would have said I was joyful if I were happy about my life circumstances. Of course, I wasn't happy about health issues that arose, the death of family members, my divorce, or other life transitions. The question is not are you happy but are you choosing joy.

"Life is a gift from God. Every day, we have the opportunity to unwrap the gift of abundant life. How we use that gift, and how we feel about it, all comes down to perspective. Yesterday, today, and tomorrow are all gifts. No matter what happens—if we lose our job, a family member, friend, or good health—we have a choice in how we respond. We can dwell only on the pain, the unfairness, or the uncertainty. Or we can look beyond those to catch a glimmer of joy that is always present."[57]

Are you choosing joy? Are you choosing to lean in to the everlasting, loving arms of Jesus? Are you choosing joy? For it is possible to feel sad and the joy of the Lord at the same time. The last year and a half I felt immense grief when my fifty-three-year-old brother lost his battle with cancer, and my mother passed the following year. That was an immense amount of grief condensed into a short period of time. I found that you can't rush the grieving process. It has to run its course. Sometimes, as you go through the stages of grief you may repeat a couple of the steps as healing takes place one layer at a time. Maybe you feel as if you were healed in a certain area of your life, and yet here you are again. It may be that you are going a little deeper and receiving another layer, perhaps a deeper level of healing.

People shared with me that losing your mother is different from losing other family members. That is true, for after all, she is your *mother*. Every day I miss my mom, and every day I praise the Lord for all that she has taught me and the great example she was. No matter what came up, my mother would always remind us of God's faithfulness and of his might and strength. So every day I feel sad, and every day I rejoice that my mother and my brother are with their Lord and Savior. Thank you, Jesus!

It seems like an oxymoron that the seeds of grief planted in the soil of life storms would sprout and flourish into God's joy. We know that our meter in our joy tank has different readings. "Dear brothers and sisters, when troubles of any kind come your way, consider it an opportunity for great joy" (James 1:2).

How would you describe your joy tank at the moment?

_____

At varying times, we are running on empty, dependent on others, or filled to the brim. When you choose to desire God and find your delight in him, you will find *joy*. When we delight in God, we are living in accordance with his Word and desiring him above all else. Nothing will ever compare to that.

We want to choose *joy* because a joy-filled life pleases God and brings honor to him. As we surrender to and pursue God, he will infuse us with his joy. God wants us to find all our peace, joy, and happiness in him, for that brings glory and honor to him.

"Obey God and leave all the consequences to Him."[58]

Challenger Deep

According to Psalm 43:4, who is our joy and delight?

_____

What question does Galatians 4:15 ask us about joy?

_____

Did you ever have joy? Where did it go? Has something or someone stolen your joy?

_____

If you feel like you need to have your joy restored, read and ponder Psalm 51:12. When was the last time that you asked God to fill you with joy?

_____

God want us to be full of joy. He wants our joy to be restored. God wants us to live full joyful lives.

Ocean Trenches

Write out a couple of journal entries to record your answers to these questions:

- What are some things that distract you from joy?

_____

_____

- Who or what has stolen your joy?

_____

_____

If you feel like there is a slow leak in your joy tank or that it empties out just as fast as it is filled, reflect upon just a few joy verses. You may also choose to memorize or journal one of these verses.

- Rejoice in the Lord always. I will say it again: Rejoice! (Philippians 4:4 NIV)
- Then I will go to the altar of God, to God, my joy and my delight. (Psalm 43:4 NIV)
- Rejoice in the Lord. (Philippians 3:1)
- When he prays to God, he will be accepted. And God will receive him with joy and restore him to good standing. (Job 33:26)
- You make known to me the path of life; you will fill me with joy in your presence, with eternal pleasures at your right hand. (Psalm 16:11 NIV)

Two Sides of Joy—Feeling and an Action

Let's dive a little deeper into joy and take notice of the differences between joy and happiness.

Joy is a little word. Happiness is a bigger word.

Joy is in the heart. Happiness is on the face.

Joy is of the soul. Happiness is of the moment.

A.W . Tozer said, "George Mueller would not preach until his heart was happy in the grace of God; Ian Ruybroeck would not write while his feelings were low but would retire to a quiet place and wait on God till he felt the spirit of inspiration. The Christian owes it to the world to be supernaturally joyful."[59]

Haydn, the great composer, was once asked why his church music was so cheerful, and he replied, "When I think upon God, my heart is so full of joy that the notes dance and leap, as it were, from my pen; and since God has given me a cheerful heart, it will be pardoned me that I serve Him with a cheerful spirit."[60]

Are we happy? Are we joyful? Are we wearing the garment of sackcloth and wailing, or are we wearing the garment of joy and praising?

Sea Surface

Here is an example of wailing: "When Mordecai learned of all that had been done, he tore his clothes, put on sackcloth and ashes, and went out into the city, wailing loudly and bitterly" (Esther 4:1 NIV).

Sackcloth was an uncomfortable material worn in times of grieving or to show repentance for sin.

What would you identify as a current or recent wailing?

_____

Are you wearing a rough, gloomy sackcloth, or are you wearing a colorful, celebratory garment of praise?

_____

Challenger Deep

Yahweh provides restoration as we choose to redirect our gaze from our pain, grief, and anger to our Redeemer. As we choose God, joy, and obedience, we transition from wearing a garment of sackcloth and wailing to wearing a garment of praise and being joyful. Surrender your pain, grief, or anger to the faithful restorer. We will discover that our restoration is ongoing. In some areas of healing we are further along than we think, and in other areas we are still in need of healing.

Using a scale of 1 to 5, identify your growth status as of today.

1 – a current pressing need

2 – something that you can relate to from the past

3 – something you have dealt with in the past but find there is another layer of healing

4 – an area where the Holy Spirit is speaking to your heart

5 – does not apply

1	2	3	4	5	A painful situation
1	2	3	4	5	An area of loss
1	2	3	4	5	Deep grief
1	2	3	4	5	Anger over circumstances
1	2	3	4	5	Anger over the outcome
1	2	3	4	5	Angry with a person
1	2	3	4	5	Angry with yourself
1	2	3	4	5	Angry with God

Ocean Trenches

Identify a pain point that you will surrender to God.

_____

Identify a loss/grief that you will ask the Lord to heal.

_____

Identify an area of anger that you will repent of and release to the Lord.

_____

When we release our burdens to the Lord with a surrendered heart, mind, and soul, we will feel free. Let us sing songs of praise!

The Expositor's Bible Commentary has this to say about Psalm 30:12 (NIV): "'that my heart may sing your praises and not be silent. Lord my God, I will praise you forever.' The Lord was faithful in changing circumstances. He is the Lord who effectually changed wailing into dancing, mourning into joy, and a deathly cry into a song of joy. Such is the goodness of God. Because of the mercy of the Lord, the psalmist vows to continue in the praise of God. The NIV translates 'glory' (kābôd) as 'heart.' The word occurs in parallelism with 'soul' and so frequently refers to the whole human being or existence. He will glorify the Lord!"[61]

Write your praises in your journal or sing praise to your Savior, Redeemer, restorer. For he is a faithful and merciful God.

Glorify the Lord, praise his name for all that he has done.

Praise him for all he has done that you know nothing about.

Thank him for protecting you from what could have happened.

Praise him for sending the resources you needed.

Glorify him for providing counsel.

Praise him for godly friends.

Praise him for giving you the strength to set up healthy boundaries.

Glorify him for teaching you to say no.

Praise him for changing the circumstances.

Praise him for not changing the circumstances but changing you.

Praise him for his guidance.

Thank him for his mercy.

Praise him today and forever!

Joy Challenge to Measure Your Joy Tank

When is the last time you had a good challenge? Some of you may say, "Yes, bring it on." This challenge will bring such an amazing, joyous outcome you may want to incorporate this challenge into a daily, weekly, or monthly habit or goal. Ready? Let's go fill up your joy tank.

Sea Surface

Here is a Monthly Joy Challenge: Each day, read one verse and write the joy you find there. I have started the first couple of days. Ready, set, go!

Day	Scripture	Joy Statement
1	Joy for the grace of God	2 Corinthians 9:8
2	Joy for the love of God for each of us	John 15:9–11
3		Psalm 30:11
4		Isaiah 40:31
5		James 1:2–4
6		Psalm 19:8
7		John 3:16
8		Philippians 4:9
9		John 15:1–7
10		Proverbs 17:6
11		Romans 8:28
12		Isaiah 35:10
13		2 Timothy 1:8–10

14		Galatians 5:22–23
15		Romans 15:13
16		Isaiah 12:6
17		Psalm 30:5
18		Philippians 4:11
19		Proverbs 10:3
20		John 16:21
21		Nehemiah 8:10
22		John 16:24
23		1 John 3:1
24		Romans 14:17
25		Proverbs 15:23
26		Romans 14:17
27		Isaiah 9:3
28		John 16:22
29		Proverbs 10:28
30		Philemon 1:7
31		Ecclesiastes 9:7

Imagine how your life could change if you read and believed a joy Scripture daily. Joy is a game changer. It is amazing how we can have a totally different perspective when we choose joy. Seek the Lord. Rejoice!

Challenger Deep

Column 1 is an acronym for REJOICE. Select and circle a word from Columns 2, 3, and 4 that best reflects your R E J O I C E. Write that word in Column 5.

Column 1	Column 2	Column 3	Column 4	Column 5
R	Repent	Restore	Redeemer	
E	Encouragement	Endurance	Edify	
J	Joy	Just	Jehovah	
O	Obedience	Overjoyed	Offering	
I	Impossible	Instruction	Integrity	
C	Choose	Care	Confidence	
E	Exalt	Everlasting	Eternal	

Ocean Trenches

Record your word selection from Column 5 to view your REJOICE selection

R _____

E _____

J _____

O _____

I _____

C _____

E _____

Seeking and Finding Joy

Joy is possible for everyone, no matter your circumstances. When you seek the pure, true joy of the Lord, you will discover a joy that is richer, purer, and deeper than you had thought. The joy of the Lord reverberates within and through us to others. Share your joys and your tears, your victories and hardships. That's what true friends do. We share life. We share the joy of the Lord.

Sometimes you break before you know it. Valerie watched as the ambulance took her thirty-year-old mother away. It had happened before so she had no idea her mother would never be back. The adults might have known. But she was only seven and, until that day, they had protected her well. Her mother's death changed everything. Where she lived, what she ate, how she spent holidays, who she called family. Mostly it changed her heart. Valerie couldn't name it at the time, but her biggest loss was the ability to trust. She no longer trusted people. She certainly didn't trust God. And she didn't care. She became angry, resentful, and reckless. Broken.

The thing about God, though, is you can give up on him, but he never gives up on you. For exactly forty years, Valerie floundered while God pursued, constantly pulling her back toward himself as she tried in vain to heal her grief on her own. He loved her even while she hated him.

Valerie and her family members each carry pieces of her mother inside. Her mother is with Jesus *and* with her. Her mother is not lost, and thanks to the grace of our Lord, Valerie is not lost either. She considers herself the one sheep of the ninety-nine—fully loved and filled with joy.

Step beyond the noise, pain, situation, people, and meet God there. He is waiting with outstretched arms for you to come. Elisabeth Elliot shares, "Among the most joyful people I have known have been some who seem to have had no human reason for joy. The sweet fragrance of Christ has shown through their lives."[62] Don't let another day pass without finding joy. Let today be the day that you rediscover joy. Embrace the joy droplet that you have and watch it grow. Let joy be the desire of your heart.

Sometimes it happens by looking at a situation from a different perspective, and there you have it—joy. Other times it is by making a decision not to lose your joy, a choice to hold on to your joy. In *Turn My Mourning into Dancing*, Henri Nouwen tells us, "Joy does not simply happen to us. We have to choose joy and keep choosing it every day."[63]

Frederick Buechner shares, "Joy is a mystery because it can happen anywhere, anytime, even under the most unpromising circumstances, even in the midst of suffering, with tears in its eyes."[64]

Sea Surface

What is your definition of joy?

_____

_____

What brings you joy?

_____

_____

How do you seek joy?

_____

_____

Challenger Deep

Christine Trimpe shares, "The joy of the Lord sustains those who know Him and spend time in His Word."[65]

True, lasting joy comes from choosing to be in the Word and in the presence of the Lord. To truly seek joy is when we seek God. We need to seek God, his wisdom, and directions and align our thoughts, plans, hopes, and dreams with him. Seeking God is seeking godly character. Joy is not fleeting as it does not depend on our circumstances or how we feel. Choose joy today. Choose to trust every detail of your life to the capable and loving heavenly Father.

"Be joyful in hope, patient in affliction, faithful in prayer" (Romans 12:12 NIV).

When we choose joy, we are trusting God with our life. Do you trust God enough to lay down your big messy life in the hands of your Savior? When we choose joy, we are choosing not to respond to the outward circumstance. How have you responded in the past that did not reflect joy? When we choose joy, we are choosing to trust God and find contentment. When we choose joy, we are choosing the strength of the Lord and not our own. When we choose joy, we are not choosing what we think others can give us. When we choose joy, we are not settling for what we think can make us happy. When we choose joy, we are not settling for living by our ever-changing feelings.

So, what is your normal route in choosing joy?

_____

_____

Ocean Trenches

True joy, not temporary happiness, can only be found in our relationship with God.

Read the following seek Scripture verses.

1. You will seek me and find me when you seek me with all your heart. (Jeremiah 29:13 NIV)
2. Look to the Lord and his strength; seek his face always. (1 Chronicles 16:11 NIV)
3. You, God, are my God, earnestly I seek you; I thirst for you, my whole being longs for you, in a dry and parched land where there is no water. (Psalm 63:1 NIV)
4. Ask and it will be given to you; seek and you will find; knock and the door will be opened to you. (Matthew 7:7 NIV)
5. Take delight in the Lord, and he will give you the desires of your heart. (Psalm 37:4 NIV)
6. I sought the Lord, and he answered me; he delivered me from all my fears. (Psalm 34:4 NIV)
7. Seek the Lord while he may be found; call on him while he is near. (Isaiah 55:6 NIV)
8. Look to the Lord and his strength; seek his face always. (Psalm 105:4 NIV)
9. Blessed are those who keep his statutes and seek him with all their heart. (Psalm 119:2 NIV)
10. Glory in his holy name; let the hearts of those who seek the Lord rejoice. (1 Chronicles 16:10 NIV)

Based on these seek verses,

Whom shall we seek? _____

How shall we seek? _____

When shall we seek? _____

Where shall we seek? _____

Why should we seek? _____

What is your favorite seek verse? _____

Yet I will rejoice in the Lord! I will be joyful in the God of my salvation! (Habakkuk 3:18)

Triumphant Joy

We experience true joy not because of our circumstances or anything we have done, but because of our personal relationship with God. It's a joy that does not change, for it is a lasting, triumphant joy. When we go through hard times with a barrage of difficult circumstances, we discover fertile soil for joy if we choose to trust God and rejoice in the Lord.

Yes, life is hard. We suffer in unfair situations, experience deep disappointments, deal with betrayal, experience physical pain, etc. But when we choose to shift our focus to God, when we seek him and step out in faith, we discover triumphant joy.

Ruth Chou Simons, in *Fields of Joy*, shares, "Tell your soul what to do—to rejoice in what is true. God's faithfulness drives you to further dependence on His Word and a greater cultivation of lasting joy."[66] Discover triumphant joy dependent on the one and only joy giver.

> Discover triumphant joy dependent on the one and only joy giver.

"The joy of the Lord cannot flow from us without the Holy Spirit dwelling in us."[67]

Sea Surface

How do you change your focus from a problem to God?

_____

_____

List a favorite promise from God that you hold to during trying times.

_____

_____

List a Scripture that is meaningful to you during pressing or waiting seasons.

_____

Challenger Deep

You can choose joy because of your personal relationship with God. Your joy is not based on your circumstances. When you experience joy, you discover true joy overcomes the hardships and disappointments of life. Happiness depends on circumstances. Joy depends on our relationship with Jesus Christ. Choose joy. Decide today if you are going to live by your circumstances or live as a godly believer in relationship with God. When we turn our gaze to our Savior Jesus Christ, we can be triumphant over our situation and rejoice in the Lord. Triumphant joy is recorded in Philippians 4:13–18. Paul praised God for the opportunity to further the gospel through his time in prison. Paul encouraged others to go out and preach with an urgency. Paul chose joy. He did not wait until his circumstances were different or he was released from prison. We are presented with a choice in how we respond to everything that comes our way. If we truly know God, we will know the joy of the Lord and the fullness of joy.

Philippians 4 tells us to rejoice always. Yes, you may have all the reason in the world to be unhappy, but we are not seeking happy—we are seeking joy. Happy is fleeting but joy is lasting. We choose joy and to rejoice. "We can always rejoice when our eyes are fixed on the Lord."[68]

According to Philippians 4:4, rejoicing is not a one-and-done experience. It is more like always and again. "Always—even amidst the afflictions now distressing you (Philippians 1:28–30). Again—as he had already said, 'Rejoice' (Philippians 3:1)."[69]

Each day gives us the opportunity to glorify God through surrender, obedience, trust, gratefulness, believing, praising, rejoicing, etc.

What happened when you chose to rejoice even though the situation remained the same?

_____

_____

Share how a negative thought was changed to a positive thought.

_____

_____

When Carol went for her yearly mammogram, she was expecting to receive a clear report. After all, she already had breast cancer, twice. She did her time. Carol was caught off guard when she received a call back from the hospital because something looked different from the mammogram last year. Carol was devastated. "Oh, no, not again. How can this happen again? And who knows where else it has spread."

Then she remembered a friend who recently passed away who also had cancer three times. Every morning Carol's first thought was, *How many more days before I go to the hospital and find out for sure if the cancer has returned*, as she waited two weeks for her appointment.

This is when Carol realized the importance of having Scripture memorized and stored in your mind and heart to speak to your fears. When fears arose, the Lord was faithful to wash his Word over Carol's troubled mind. He replaced her concerns with his promises. "So do not fear, for I am with you; do not be dismayed, for I am your God. I will strengthen you and help you; I will uphold you with my righteous right hand" (Isaiah 41:10 NIV).

The news was very upsetting and yet Carol had peace. She trusted God that whatever the outcome he would be with her. The night before she was to return to the hospital, she slept like a baby. God knew she needed the physical rest. The next morning, the technician brought her in for the additional views. To Carol's astonishment, the tech announced there was no change in the mammogram from last year. There was *no cancer*. What a relief. Carol was standing on God's promises and trusting his plan. God reminded her that he is sovereign and nothing can happen to her unless he allows it.

It is truly amazing how we can experience peace and joy at the same time we are dealing with stressful situations, especially when we are unsure of the outcome.

Our joy is not based on our circumstances or our positive attitude but our joy is the joy of the Lord. The Lord resides in our lives, and joy reigns in our hearts. Even when going through sorrowful days and excruciating emotional pain, the Lord is with us at all times, always. We can rejoice always.

Ocean Trenches

We have joy because God has been faithful in the past, is faithful in our today, and will be faithful in our future.

How has God been faithful in the past?

_____

_____

How is God faithful today?

_____

_____

How will God be faithful in the future?

_____

_____

STRENGTH
in Thriving and Flourishing

Thrive with resiliency
and you will flourish
BEYOND;
God is always faithful
to carry you
to a place BEYOND.

Resilient

When you hear the word resilient, does a certain person come to mind? A friend who always seems to bounce back and adjust no matter what comes her way? We may view that person as the resilient one, but biblical resiliency is displayed when we show faith in difficult circumstances.

We learn resiliency when we travel with Jesus through the storm and give him all the glory and praise. A resilient faith is able to see us through our hard times and come out stronger on the other side. Even when we feel like the odds are against us and we do not have the strength or bandwidth to fight this battle, Exodus 14:14 reminds us that the Lord will fight for us. God is always working on our behalf.

> Resilient faith builds strength we didn't know was possible.

When we are feeling weary and battle worn, the Lord gives us his strength in his way and his time. Resilient faith builds strength we didn't know was possible.

Sea Surface

We have had things taken away from us, and we have had things not turn out as we had expected. But during those times we can become strong, resilient, obedient women as we choose to trust and hope in God.

> When we are feeling weary and battle worn, the Lord gives us his strength in his way and his time.

Here are just a couple of examples of biblical characters who displayed resiliency.

JOB

In Job 1, we read all that was taken from Job. List two things he lost.

    1. _____

    2. _____

"In all of this, Job did not sin by blaming God" (Job 1:22).

    What did Job not do? _____

"Then Job replied to the Lord: I know that you can do anything, and no one can stop you" (Job 42:1–2).

Can we agree with Job? If so, write *Amen!* _____

"The Lord blessed the latter part of Job's life more than the former part" (Job 42:12 NIV).

HABAKKUK

In Habakkuk 3:17–18, we read, "Even though the fig trees have no blossoms, and there are no grapes on the vines; . . . even though the flocks die in the fields, and the cattle barns are empty, yet I will rejoice in the Lord! I will be joyful in the God of my salvation!"

We all have experienced a time when something did not go according to our plan or what we had hoped for. It is important to name it. But what is even more important is how we react, how we dealt with it.

Share if you have had an opportunity to choose to be more resilient.

_____

_____

The reward for obedience is incomparable. Choose joy. Choose God. Choose to be strong and resilient.

Grace's life hit a new level of stress as she dealt with three traumatic life storms simultaneously. She was worried about her family's finances as their income was suddenly cut in half due to a job loss. Grace was lovingly serving as health proxy for her sister who was dying of Huntington's disease. She was also consumed with the thoughts of her son's safety as he was deployed to Iraq. Because of the unsurmountable stress levels associated with these storms, Grace's body responded violently by developing chronic fibromyalgia, a painful, debilitating disease. Her entire body ached, her joints and arms felt like they were going to crumble, and she wailed. Pain at this level affected every area of her life with no relief in sight. When the fibromyalgia would flare up, she would get depressed over dealing with the chronic pain. Grace was so grateful to God for providing her a counselor and meeting their financial needs throughout the years. As she walked this uncharted path, she would journal, read the Bible, and watch as much Christian television as possible. If she woke up during the night, she asked the Lord to be her first thought as she opened her eyes, and he was. God's peace enveloped her, and she was able to go back to sleep. God's peace continued to flow through every area of her life, even the parts that were in limbo. Even when things got worse before they got better. God was always faithful. God has been faithful in the past, and his faithfulness continues for whatever may come. Her life verse is Romans 8:28, "And we know that God causes everything to work together for the good of those who love God and are called according to his purpose for them." With each day, with each storm, God is building resilience in her life, and she truly knows the strength of the Lord.

Challenger Deep

Let's look at some of the character qualities that are found in being resilient.

STRENGTH: Because we have surrendered our weaknesses and relied on God, we have a newfound strength. We have become strong.

- Be strong and courageous, all you who put your hope in the Lord! (Psalm 31:24)
- Be strong in the Lord and in his mighty power. (Ephesians 6:10)

How has waiting on the Lord built resiliency in your life?

_____

_____

How have you become resilient as you relied on God's strength?

_____

_____

TRUST: We choose to trust God at all times, whether we understand the reason or not.

- "Trusting God means looking beyond what we can see to what God sees."[70]
- Trust in the Lord with all your heart, and do not lean on your own understanding. (Proverbs 3:5 ESV)
- Trust in him at all times. (Psalm 62:8)
- "We must trust God with what we can't control."[71]

How does trust build your resiliency?

_____

_____

What are the disadvantages of trusting and leaning on our own understanding?

_____

_____

THANKFULNESS:

- Always be joyful. Never stop praying. Be thankful in all circumstances, for this is God's will for you who belong to Christ Jesus. (1 Thessalonians 5:16–18)
- And give thanks for everything to God the Father in the name of our Lord Jesus Christ. (Ephesians 5:20)

What can you give thanks for today?

_____

_____

How does giving thanks become a building block of resiliency?

_____

_____

HUMILITY: Being humble is another quality of the resilient life.

- Humble yourselves before the Lord. (James 4:10)
- I know what it is to be in need, and I know what it is to have plenty. (Philippians 4:12 NIV)

Give an example of how you were able to humble yourself.

_____

_____

What are the strengths of being humble?

_____

_____

FAITH: We exchange our fear for our faith.

- For God gave us a spirit not of fear but of power and love and self-control. (2 Timothy 1:7 ESV)
- Be watchful, stand firm in the faith, act like men, be strong. (1 Corinthians 16:13 ESV)

Where have you exchanged your fear for faith?

_____

_____

Share a faith-building moment that propelled resiliency.

_____

_____

CONQUERORS: Through Jesus Christ, we are more than conquerors.

- We are afflicted in every way, but not crushed; perplexed, but not driven to despair; persecuted, but not forsaken; struck down, but not destroyed. (2 Corinthians 4:8–9 ESV)

- No, in all these things we are more than conquerors through him who loved us. (Romans 8:37 ESV)

How has God demonstrated his faithfulness recently?

_____

_____

How has being a conqueror built your resiliency?

_____

_____

PEACE: Receive the peace that passes all understanding from the Prince of Peace.

- I have said these things to you, that in me you may have peace. In the world you will have tribulation. But take heart; I have overcome the world. (John 16:33 ESV)

Describe a time where your heart, soul, and mind were covered in a blanket of peace.

_____

_____

How has peace become a quiet strength and resiliency?

_____

_____

COURAGE: Our courage comes from the Lord.

- Be strong, and let your heart take courage, all you who wait for the Lord! (Psalm 31:24 ESV)
- Wait patiently for the Lord. Be brave and courageous. Yes, wait patiently for the Lord. (Psalm 27:14).

Share a moment when God encouraged you to take a bold, brave step.

_____

_____

POWER: We are filled with the power of the Holy Spirit.

- He gives power to the faint, and to him who has no might he increases strength. (Isaiah 40:29 ESV)

When has God empowered you?

_____

_____

STEADFASTNESS: Be strong and immovable.

- Always work enthusiastically for the Lord, for you know that nothing you do for the Lord is ever useless. (1 Corinthians 15:58)

We all have a blend of both strengths and weaknesses. What is an area of strength, where you are immovable and steadfast?

_____

_____

Where would you like to challenge yourself to be steadfast?

_____

_____

Ocean Trenches

"One of the most remarkable things about human beings is how resilient we can be. Yet one of the most surprising things about human beings is how all that resilience can evaporate in a moment."[72]

Which of these resilient characteristics is your strongest?

_____

_____

Write a character description of yourself before the storm.

_____

_____

_____

_____

Write a character description of yourself after the storm.

_____

_____

_____

_____

Restored by Grace

God is the giver and restorer of life. When we experience deep loss and all seems to have been taken from our life, God restores. When we are in the thick of things, we often feel as though our pain will never end and loss will be our permanent address. Our suffering will not last forever. "Though you have made me see troubles, many and bitter, you will restore my life again" (Psalm 71:20 NIV).

"When in a storm, Jesus calls us to ante up and choose to find our faith and make a choice to boldly hold on tight."[73]

Read the five verses below and underline what will be restored.

- I will restore to you the years that the swarming locust has eaten. (Joel 2:25 ESV)
- Restore to me the joy of your salvation, and make me willing to obey you. (Psalm 51:12)
- For I will restore you to health and heal your wounds. (Jeremiah 30:17 NIV)
- He restores my soul. He leads me in paths of righteousness for his name's sake. (Psalm 23:3 ESV)
- After you have suffered for a little while, the God of all grace, who called you to His eternal glory in Christ, will Himself perfect, confirm, strengthen, and establish you. (1 Peter 5:10 NASB)

God himself will *perfect* or *restore* you. The giver of life, the God of all grace, the God who has called us, he himself will restore, repair, or adjust us. He will make us ready for

The giver of life, the God of grace, the God who has called us, he himself will restore, repair, or adjust us. He will make us ready for who, what, and how he wants us to be, for our good and for his glory.

who, what, and how he wants us to be, for our good and for his glory. He will perfect us even with all our inadequacies and deficiencies and make us fully prepared for each day and assignment that he has for us. God, our restorer makes us complete and whole.

How has the Lord perfected you, restored you, in spite of your inadequacies or because of your deficiencies, and brought you to a place where you could move forward or complete that task?

_____

_____

God himself will *confirm* or *secure* you. God will confirm and give you support where you feel shaky. At times the Holy Spirit will lead you in a certain direction.

Please write and/or share when:

You felt a prompting to go in certain direction.

_____

_____

You felt a prompting to do something very purposeful and intentional.

_____

_____

The Holy Spirit gave you a confirmation to say or do something very specific.

_____

_____

The Holy Spirit gave you a confirmation not to say or do anything.

_____

_____

God himself will *strengthen* you. God strengthens us spiritually and physically so that we can withstand the trials and storms of life. "You can be defeated by life's unavoidable disappointments, or you can become stronger because of them."[74]

How would you measure your strength before and after your unexpected storm?

_____

_____

God himself will *establish* you. You will feel settled as you feel secure on God's firm foundation.

Explain how or why you feel more established, settled, or secure as you stand on a firm foundation.

_____

_____

God is our divine aid as he himself perfects, confirms, strengthens, and establishes us. Life storms have a way of catapulting us into a major growth spurt in our life and more specifically in our calling. Usually, what we are experiencing today is in preparation for tomorrow. Sometimes, it doesn't have to be a major storm, it may be adjusting our sail so that we are headed in a direction that God has planned for us.

Sea Surface

God has called you. "He will complete what he has begun. The Divine act of calling us to that glory contains the earnest, that everything will so come to pass as to take us forward to the end of the calling. In His power, for His sake and by His word.[75]

Reflect upon a time when God had you change course.

_____

_____

What life lessons do we learn when we choose to be obedient to what God has for us?

_____

_____

Where have you seen the most growth?

_____

"May he equip you with all you need for doing his will. May he produce in you, through the power of Jesus Christ, every good thing that is pleasing to him. All glory to him forever and ever! Amen" (Hebrews 13:21).

Challenger Deep

As we travel through life's journey, we will experience all kinds of weather, from the perfect beach day to tsunamis. And yet in both settings, God is with us. In both settings we learn and grow.

Come to the God of all grace today and write or say a prayer. Pray and agree with the Lord to accomplish all that he has planned.

_____

_____

Praise the Lord for establishing a firm and secure foundation.

_____

_____

Praise the Lord for equipping and empowering you to serve.

_____

_____

Ocean Trenches

It has been said that the soil of suffering is fertile for growth. Often we recognize growth when we are empathetic because we can relate to another person's pain. Another area of growth is endurance as we travel the long road of suffering. Trust and hope are also growth opportunities as we hang on to our Lord and Savior.

Share what promises you have held on to during your journey.

_____

_____

Share what you hold on to for your future.

_____

_____

What areas of your life do you see grow?

_____

_____

In what area of your life would you like deeper growth?

_____

_____

Sing a song of praise to the glory of God!

Subsiding Storms and their Seasons

There are various tiers to a storm: before the storm, during the storm, and after the storm. Where are you now?

Before the storm: Before we received that health diagnosis, before our spouse left, before our family member passed, before our financial resources were depleted. Then, out of nowhere, boom. We have been knocked down.

During the storm: The storm has hit us hard. How do we weather the storm with its tumultuous waters and fierce winds that have rocked our world? By the grace of God, he walks with us through the storm. We push forward through the losses, setbacks, and agonizing circumstances. We align with God's purpose for our life. We discover gratitude is everything. Gratitude for what you have and that God will carry you through is key to surviving tragedy.

After the storm: Go through the storm. Yes, not only survive the storm but thrive. This empowers us to flourish thereafter. We find a renewed hope and reclaim our passion for life. We experience fulfillment and joy in a more authentic and deeper way. We have discovered and learned invaluable insights.

Sea Surface

As you travel through your unexpected storm, you may find yourself surprised that you have also received unexpected blessings and lessons along the way. "These trials will show that your faith is genuine. It is being tested as fire tests and purifies gold—though your faith is far more precious than mere gold. So when your faith remains strong through many trials, it will bring much praise and glory and honor on the day when Jesus Christ is revealed to the whole world" (1 Peter 1:7).

What blessings and lessons does this verse tell you about your faith?

_____

_____

What is the outcome of remaining strong through many trials?

_____

_____

Share an unexpected blessing you received as a result of remaining faithful.

_____

_____

"Dear brothers and sisters, when troubles of any kind come your way, consider it an opportunity for great joy. For you know that when your faith is tested, your endurance has a chance to grow. So let it grow, for when your endurance is fully developed, you will be perfect and complete, needing nothing" (James 1:2–4).

What happens when our faith is tested?

_____

_____

How has your endurance been developed?

_____

_____

Challenger Deep

Each tier of your storm will bring about change, challenges, and unexpected blessings that you could not have imagined. "For everything there is a season, a time for every activity under heaven" (Ecclesiastes 3:1).

After the storm, when the winds have died down and the water is smooth, we enter a hush season, as though the storm is forgotten. Our life returns to routine. We want to cultivate a perpetual growth pattern, not only during the storms but also in the quiet routine days. Why? "So that you may live a life worthy of the Lord and please him in every way: bearing fruit in every good work, growing in the knowledge of God" (Colossians 1:10 NIV).

How do we live a life worthy of the Lord?

_____

_____

How can we please him and bear fruit?

_____

_____

Give a few examples of how we can grow in the knowledge of God.

_____

_____

Ocean Trenches

"Do your best to present yourself to God as one approved, a worker who does not need to be ashamed and who correctly handles the word of truth" (2 Timothy 2:15 NIV). As we continue to grow in the Lord, we may be entering a new season, a new level, a spiritual growth spurt.

How do we grow in a deeper way?

_____

_____

God is preparing you for something new, beyond what you have done or been before, perhaps something bigger and greater than you've had in the past.

Share that dream, even if you only have a glimpse of what that might look like.

_____

_____

Do you feel stretched beyond your comfort zone? Keep the faith. Hold on to the truth of God's Word and claim his promises over your life. For you are victorious in Christ.

How is God preparing you for your season of growth?

_____

_____

Storms and Moving the Aftermath

Near the New England coastline, there is always a group of born-and-raised ocean-storm chasers who welcome storms and hurricane seasons with open arms. They arrive at the ocean with their hopes as high as the billowing waves, ready, willing, and able to glimpse flashes of lightning illuminating the sand, sea, and sky. They watch and wait to get a view of the fleeting majestic display of power and beauty.

After the storm, that same majestic landscape is now painted with smelly seaweed and accompanied by debris of broken shells, rocks, bottles, etc. carried to shore from tumultuous waves.

That is when we are grateful to see the town beachcomber ride along the shoreline collecting the seaweed and debris. After our life storm has subsided, we are not necessarily responsible for cleaning up the aftermath for everyone who was involved in the storm. We are not called to be a beachcomber picking up everyone's trash.

God is with us always and will continue to be with us after the storm as well. It is God who will deal with the debris and the aftermath of the storm. The Lord brought us through the storm, carried us, and will continue to walk us through each season of life. We can choose our growth pattern. Do we want to stay stuck in our past? Have we planted our feet in the quicksand of today, or do we desire to continue moving, continue growing, continue learning to be all that God has created us to be? Life is a process. We need to stay focused on living through the process with our heart, mind, and soul anchored in Christ alone.

Sea Surface

Write out a prayer or a declaration statement proclaiming where you want to stand—stuck in the past, planted in today, or moving and growing today and every day that the Lord gives you.

_____

_____

Look up the song "In Christ Alone" and share how the lyrics and melody speak to your heart today.

_____

_____

Is there another song that has a special meaning to you today?

_____

_____

Is there a Scripture that has special meaning to you today?

_____

_____

Challenger Deep

We have navigated in different directions and shifted from our pain point to our purpose point. We are hopeful to see what exciting things the Lord has planned for us and through us.

Read the following purpose Scriptures and think about how they speak to you today.

- I know that you can do anything, and no one can stop you. (Job 42:2)
- You can make many plans, but the Lord's purpose will prevail. (Proverbs 19:21)

Write or say a prayer and ask the Lord to align your desires with the plans he has for your life.

_____

_____

Healing and growth take place when we shift our pain to our purpose. When we go through our test, our trial, being hurt or experiencing a setback or huge disappointment provides an opportunity for growth and to trust God at a deeper level. We can recognize that we have made progress and are now at a different place. God has moved us onto a healthier place—a safe place—and we want to keep on keeping on.

We want to move on with God to our next destination, our next assignment. We know that God knows where we have been. God knows where we are going. God has provided for us in the past and will continue to do so in the future. At this stage, we are no longer at the same point as when the storm hit, and hopefully we have moved beyond.

Ocean Trenches

What new thing is God doing in your life?

_____

_____

Do you have a sense of something new that God is calling you to? If so, write out a purpose statement of what you sense God is calling you to.

_____

_____

Continue to pray for your new adventure with God. Have your prayer partners join you in prayer as your support beams.

From Surviving to Thriving through the Storm

We learned that the only way to survive the storm was to go through the storm. There had to be movement. Somedays God carried you, and other days God gave you the steps. You moved on through the storm and survived. Not only did you survive but you also thrived.

Sea Surface

Here are some biblical principles that most likely you have learned as you went through the storm. I strongly encourage you to continue incorporating them as daily habits so they are well established!

- Acknowledge where you are.
- Seek God for direction.
- Develop a plan to move forward.
- Obey God's plan each step of the way.
- Stand on God's promises.
- Seek community for prayer and support.

Which of these principles do you consider most valuable?

_____
_____

Which of these principles would you like to work on a little more?

_____
_____

What else would you add to this list?

_____
_____

Challenger Deep

Here are a few suggestions to assist you in creating new daily habits.

- Seek an accountability partner.
- Schedule a time in your planner or phone to pray.
- Schedule a time in your planner or phone to read the Bible.
- Write in a journal what you believe God is leading you to do.
- Write out a new promise each day, week, or month and meditate on that promise.

Ocean Trenches

Perhaps the Lord is leading you in a new direction. Maybe the Lord is opening an opportunity for you in preparation for your next God adventure. What might God be preparing you for? Seek his direction. Wait. Seek godly wisdom.

Proverbs 4:7 (ESV) tells us, "The beginning of wisdom is this: Get wisdom." Do you need wisdom in decision-making, leadership, insight, listening skills, communication skills, etc.? God will give you what you need to complete the assignment he has given you. God will give you the knowledge. Wisdom is the application of the knowledge. God will give you the stamina, insight, and confidence to move through these next steps. Continue to apply the new strength and confidence that God has taught you.

Write out or speak the following prayer:

Dear heavenly Father, I thank you that you are forever faithful and that you have brought me through the storm. Thank you for the things you have taught me. Thank you for the courage and strength you have instilled in me. May I be forever a student and come to you daily to bask in your presence, worship you, and seek you above all else. Lord, I pray that you will give me:

insight beyond my natural eyesight,

ears to listen beyond just hearing,

a mouth to communicate beyond my natural ability to communicate,

a mouth to be quiet when you want to speak beyond what is necessary,

physical stamina beyond my natural physical ability,

intellectual knowledge beyond my natural brain bandwidth,

and wisdom led by the power and guidance of the Holy Spirit.

May all be done to the Glory of your name. Amen!

By the grace of God we have survived. We continue to thrive not only in spite of the storm but because of the storm. We may have small setbacks or feel an emotional trigger, but that doesn't mean we are not healed. It means we are human. We become stronger with each experience. We have moved past just surviving and we are now thriving. We are declaring that we will continue to grow and flourish in the Lord. It is God's desire that we do not merely exist before, during, or after our storms but that we continue to grow, develop, and flourish in every way, every day, to the glory of his name! "May the Lord cause you to flourish, both you and your children" (Psalm 115:14 NIV).

Appendix A: Refuge Scriptures

- I will say of the Lord, "He is my refuge and my fortress, my God, in whom I trust." (Psalm 91:2 NIV)
- The eternal God is your refuge, and underneath are the everlasting arms. (Deuteronomy 33:27 NIV)
- The wise are cautious and avoid danger; fools plunge ahead with reckless confidence. (Proverbs 14:16)
- The name of the Lord is a fortified tower; the righteous run to it and are safe. (Proverbs 18:10 NIV)
- He alone is my refuge, my place of safety; he is my God, and I trust him. (Psalm 91:2)
- God is . . . my shield and the horn of my salvation, my stronghold. (Psalm 18:2 NIV)
- My victory and honor come from God alone. He is my refuge, a rock where no enemy can reach me. (Psalm 62:7)
- The Lord gives his people strength. He is a safe fortress for his anointed king. (Psalm 28:8)
- He is my loving ally and my fortress, my tower of safety, my rescuer. (Psalm 144:2)
- God's way is perfect. All the Lord's promises prove true. He is a shield for all who look to him for protection. (2 Samuel 22:31)
- My victory and honor come from God alone. He is my refuge, a rock where no enemy can reach me. (Psalm 62:7)

Appendix B: Burden Scriptures

- Praise be to the Lord, to God our Savior, who daily bears our burdens. (Psalm 68:19 NIV)
- Take my yoke upon you. Let me teach you, because I am humble and gentle at heart, and you will find rest for your souls. For my yoke is easy to bear, and the burden I give you is light. (Matthew 11:29–30)
- He comforts us in all our troubles so that we can comfort others. When they are troubled, we will be able to give them the same comfort God has given us. (2 Corinthians 1:4)
- For the Lord your God is living among you. He is mighty savior. He will take delight in you with gladness. With his love, he will calm all your fears. He will rejoice over you with joyful songs. (Zephaniah 3:17)
- Give your burdens to the Lord, and he will take care of you. He will not permit the godly to slip and fall. (Psalm 55:22)
- But in my distress I cried out to the Lord; yes, I prayed to my God for help. He heard me from his sanctuary; my cry to him reached his ears. (Psalm 18:6)
- Then call on me when you are in trouble, and I will rescue you, and you will give me glory. (Psalm 50:15)
- Share each other's burdens, and in this way obey the law of Christ. (Galatians 6:2)
- Here on earth you will have many trials and sorrows. But take heart, because I have overcome the world. (John 16:33)
- We are pressed on every side by troubles, but we are not crushed. We are perplexed, but not driven to despair. We are hunted down, but never abandoned by God. We get knocked down, but we are not destroyed. (2 Corinthians 4:8–9)

Appendix C: 30 Days of Joy Scriptures

1. Joy for the words commanded & recorded of the Lord are right. (Psalm 19:8)
2. Joy from assurance of sins forgiven. (John 3:16)
3. The love of God for each one of us. (John 15:9–11)
4. Joy because of hope. (Psalm 30:11)
5. Faith and hope despite the circumstances. (Isaiah 40:31)
6. Joy because we know goodness will come out of hardship. (Romans 8:29)
7. Joy because our character is being formed to be mature and complete. (James 1:2)
8. Joy for our confidence that Jesus can bring life out of death. (2 Timothy 1:8–10)
9. Joy for the grace God has given us. (2 Corinthians 9:8)
10. God himself is our strength. (Philippians 4:11)
11. God will meet our needs. (Philippians 4:9)
12. Joy in the Holy Spirit. (Romans 14:17)
13. Joy in obedience to God. (John 15:1–7)
14. For the fruit of the spirit. (Galatians 5:22–23)
15. When children choose well. (Proverbs 10:1)
16. The birth of a child. (John 16:21)
17. For grandchildren. (Proverbs 17:6)
18. We are called children of God. (1 John 3:1)
19. Giving joy to the heart. (Psalm 19:8)
20. Enlarged the nation and increased their joy. (Isaiah 9:3)
21. God has already approved what you do. (Ecclesiastes 9:7)
22. The prospect of the righteous is joy. (Proverbs 10:28)
23. Fill you with all you. (Romans 15:13)
24. The joy of the Lord is your strength. (Nehemiah 8:10)
25. Sing for joy for great is the Holy One. (Isaiah 12:6)
26. Your love has given me great joy and encouragement. (Philemon 1:7)
27. Everlasting joy will crown their heads. (Isaiah 35:10)
28. A person finds joy in giving an apt reply. (Proverbs 15:23)
29. You will rejoice, and no one will take away your joy. (John 16:22)
30. Weeping may stay for the night, but rejoicing comes in the morning. (Psalm 30:5)

Appendix D: One Another Scriptures (NIV)

- John 13:34 – Love One Another
- Romans 12:10 – Be Devoted to One Another
- Romans 12:16 – Harmony with One Another
- Romans 14:19 – Build Up One Another
- Romans 15:5 – Be Likeminded
- Romans 15:7 – Accept One Another
- Colossians 3:16 – Admonish One Another
- 1 Corinthians 12:25 – Care for One Another
- Galatians 5:13 – Serve One Another
- Galatians 6:2 – Bear Burdens for One Another
- Ephesians 4:32 – Forgive One Another
- Colossians 3:13 – Be Patient
- Ephesians 4:15 – Speak Truth
- Ephesians 4:32 – Kind to One Another
- 1 Peter 5:5 – Submit to One Another
- Philippians 2:4 – Look to the Interests of Others
- Colossians 3:16 – Teach One Another
- 1 Thessalonians 4:18 – Comfort One Another
- 1 Thessalonians 5:11 – Encourage One Another
- Hebrews 3:13 – Exhort One Another
- Hebrews 10:24 – Stir Up One Another
- 1 Peter 4:9 – Show Hospitality to One Another
- 1 Peter 4:10 – Serve One Another

Endnotes

1. *Merriam-Webster.com Dictionary*, s.v. "refuge," accessed November 4, 2022, https://www.merriam-webster.com/dictionary/refuge.

2. Debbie Roth, *Drenched: Only Hope in the Storm* (Enumclaw, WA: Redemption Press, 2018), 20.

3. Dr. Michelle Bengtson, *Hope Prevails Bible Study: Insights from a Doctor's Personal Journey through Depression* (Enumclaw, WA: Redemption Press, 2017), 32.

4. Robert L. Thomas, *New American Standard Hebrew-Aramaic and Greek dictionaries: Updated Edition* (Anaheim, CA: Foundation Publications, 1998), #6006 Strong Hebrew.

5. Wayne Grudem, *1 Peter: An Introduction and Commentary,* Vol. 17 of *Tyndale New Testament Commentaries*, gen. ed. Leon Morris (Downers Grove, IL: InterVarsity Press, 1988) 202.

6. Laura Acuña, *Still Becoming: Hope, Help, and Healing for the Diet-Weary Soul* (Birmingham, AL: Brookstone Publishing Group, 2022), 114.

7. James Montgomery Boice, *Psalms 42–106: An Expositional Commentary* (Grand Rapids, MI: Baker Books, 2005), 389.

8. Dr. Michelle Bengtson, *Hope Prevails Bible Study: Insights from a Doctor's Personal Journey through Depression* (Enumclaw, WA: Redemption Press, 2017), 73.

9. Lucinda Secrest McDowell, *Soul Strong: 7 Keys to a Vibrant Life* (Birmingham, AL: New Hope, 2020), xiv.

10. *Merriam-Webster.com Dictionary*, s.v. "hope," accessed November 29, 2022, https://www.merriam-webster.com/dictionary/hope.

11. Dr. Michelle Bengtson, *Hope Prevails Bible Study: Insights from a Doctor's Personal Journey through Depression* (Enumclaw, WA: Redemption Press, 2017), 27.

12. Laura Acuña, *Still Becoming: Hope, Help, and Healing for the Diet-Weary Soul* (Birmingham, AL: Brookstone Publishing Group, 2022), 111.

13. Dr. Michelle Bengtson, *Hope Prevails Bible Study: Insights from a Doctor's Personal Journey through Depression* (Enumclaw, WA: Redemption Press, 2017), 27.

14. Carol Tetzlaff, *Ezra: Unleashing the Power of Praise* (Enumclaw, WA: Redemption Press, 2021), 20.

15. Laura Acuña, *Still Becoming: Hope, Help, and Healing for the Diet-Weary Soul* (Birmingham, AL: Brookstone Publishing Group, 2022),56.

16. Allen P. Ross, "Psalms," in John F. Walvoord & Roy B. Zuck, eds., *The Bible Knowledge Commentary: An Exposition of the Scriptures, Vol. 1* (Wheaton, IL: Victor Books, 1985), 886.

17. C. S. Lewis, *Mere Christianity* (London, England: William Collins, 2012), 9.

18. Dr. David Jeremiah, *The Prayer Matrix: Plugging into the Unseen Reality* (Colorado Springs: Multnomah, 2013), 29.

19. Lucinda Secrest McDowell, *Soul Strong: 7 Keys to a Vibrant Life* (Birmingham, AL: New Hope, 2020), 76.

20. Jennifer Hand, *My Yes is on the Table: Moving from Fear to Faith* (Chicago, IL: Moody, 2022).

21. Matthew Henry, *Matthew Henry's Commentary on the Whole Bible* (Peabody, MA: Hendrickson, 1994), 935.

22. Stanley, Charles F. *Waiting on God: Strength for Today and Hope for Tomorrow.* United States: Howard Books, 2015.

23. David Walls and Max Anders, *I & II Peter, I, II & III John, Jude,* Vol. 11 of *Holman New Testament Commentary*, ed. Max Anders (Nashville, TN: Broadman & Holman, 1999), 94–95.

24. Wayne Grudem, *1 Peter: An Introduction and Commentary,* Vol. 2 of *Tyndale New Testament Commentaries*, gen. ed. Leon Morris (Downers Grove, IL: InterVarsity Press, 1988), 205.

25. John D. Barry, gen. ed., *Faithlife Study Bible* (Bellingham, WA: Lexham Press, 2012, 2016), 1 Peter 5:10.

26. Laura Acuña, *Still Becoming: Hope, Help, and Healing for the Diet-Weary Soul* (Birmingham, AL: Brookstone Publishing Group, 2022), 111.

27. F. F. Bruce, *Romans: An Introduction and Commentary,* Vol. 6 of *Tyndale New Testament Commentaries*, gen. ed. Leon Morris (Downers Grove, IL: InterVarsity Press, 1985), 127.

28. Lawrence O. Richards, *The Bible Reader's Companion,* Vol. 6 (Wheaton, IL: Victor Books, 1991), 127.

29. *Merriam-Webster.com Dictionary*, s.v. "trust," accessed October 8, 2022, https://www.merriam-webster.com/dictionary/trust.

30. *Merriam-Webster.com Dictionary*, s.v. "tidal wave," accessed October 8, 2022, https://www.merriam-webster.com/dictionary/tidal%20wave.

31. Jerry Bridges, *Trusting God* (Colorado Springs: NavPress, 2016).

32. Jerry Bridges, *Trusting God* (Colorado Springs: NavPress, 2016).

33. Jerry Bridges, *Trusting God* (Colorado Springs: NavPress, 2016).

34. John Piper, Justin Taylor, eds., *Suffering and the Sovereignty of God* (Wheaton, IL: Crossway, 2006).

35. Jerry Bridges, *Trusting God* (Colorado Springs: NavPress, 2016), 173.

36. Martin H. Manser, ed., *Dictionary of Bible Themes: The Accessible and Comprehensive Tool for Topical Studies* (Grand Rapids, MI: Zondervan, 1996).

37. Charles F. Stanley, *Can You Still Trust God?: What Happens When You Choose to Believe* (Nashville, TN: Thomas Nelson, 2021).

38. Linda Evans Shepherd, *Prayers for Every Need* (Grand Rapids, MI: Baker Publishing Group, 2022), 17.

39. Linda Evans Shepherd, *Prayers for Every Need* (Grand Rapids, MI: Baker Publishing Group, 2022).

40. Linda Evans Shepherd, *Prayers for Every Need* (Grand Rapids, MI: Baker Publishing Group, 2022), 23.

41. Linda Evans Shepherd, *Prayers for Every Need* (Grand Rapids, MI: Baker Publishing Group, 2022), 18.

42. Sheila Walsh, *The Storm Inside Study Guide: Trade the Chaos of How You Feel for the Truth of Who You Are* (Nashville, TN: Thomas Nelson, 2014), 51.

43. Sheila Walsh, *The Storm Inside Study Guide: Trade the Chaos of How You Feel for the Truth of Who You Are* (Nashville, TN: Thomas Nelson, 2014).

44. Charles F. Stanley, *In Touch Daily Readings for Devoted Living* (Atlanta, GA: In Touch Ministries, 2022).

45. Max Anders, *Galatians, Ephesians, Philippians & Colossians,* Vol. 8 of *Holman New Testament Commentary*, ed. Max Anders (Nashville, TN: Broadman & Holman, 1999), 131.

46. John R. W. Stott, *God's New Society: The Message of Ephesians* (Downers Grove, IL: InterVarsity Press, 1979), 136.

47. Warren W. Wiersbe, *Wiersbe's Expository Outlines on the New Testament* (Wheaton, IL:: Victor Books, 1992), 546–547.

48. Kenneth S. Wuest, *Wuest's Word Studies from the Greek New Testament,* Vol. 4 (Grand Rapids, MI: Eerdmans, 1997), 89.

49. H. W. Hoehner, "Ephesians," in John F. Walvoord & Roy B. Zuck, eds., *The Bible Knowledge Commentary: An Exposition of the Scriptures,* Vol. 2 (Wheaton, IL: Victor Books, 1985), 631–632.

50. Matthew Henry, *Matthew Henry's Commentary on the Whole Bible* (Peabody, MA: Hendrickson, 1994), 2312.

51. Warren W. Wiersbe, *Wiersbe's Expository Outlines on the New Testament* (Wheaton, IL: Victor Books, 1992), 547.

52. *Merriam-Webster.com Dictionary,* s.v. "doxology," accessed January 15, 2022, https://www.merriam-webster.com/dictionary/doxology.

53. "Eph. 3:20–21," *Lexham Context Commentary: New Testament,* Vol. 2, ed. Douglas Mangum (Bellingham, WA: Lexham Press, 2020).

54. Matthew Henry, *Matthew Henry's Commentary on the Whole Bible* (Peabody, MA: Hendrickson, 1994), 781.

55. *Merriam-Webster.com Dictionary,* s.v. "joy," accessed November 7, 2022, https://www.merriam-webster.com/dictionary/joy.

56. Adria Wilkins, *The Joy Box Journal* (New York: Hachette Book Group, 2019), 35.

57. Adria Wilkins, *The Joy Box Journal* (New York: Hachette Book Group, 2019), 5.

58. Charles F. Stanley, *In Step with God: Understanding His Ways and Plans for Your Life* (Nashville, TN: Thomas Nelson, 2010), 115.

59. Paul Lee Tan, *Encyclopedia of 7700 Illustrations: Signs of the Times* (Dallas, TX: Bible Communications, 1996) 679.

60. Paul Lee Tan, *Encyclopedia of 7700 Illustrations: Signs of the Times* (Dallas, TX: Bible Communications, 1996) 679.

61. Willem A. VanGemeren, *Psalms,* Vol. 5 of *The Expositor's Bible Commentary: Revised Edition,* gen. eds. Tremper Longman III & David E. Garland (Grand Rapids, MI: Zondervan, 2008), 300–301.

62. Elisabeth Elliot, *Secure in the Everlasting Arms: Trusting the God Who Never Leaves Your Side* (Grand Rapids, MI: Baker Publishing Group, 2021).

63. Henri Nouwen, *Turn My Mourning Into Dancing: Finding Hope in Hard Times* (Nashville, TN: Thomas Nelson, 2010).

64. Frederick Buechner, *The Hungering Dark* (New York: Harper Collins, 1985).

65. Christine Trimpe, *Seeking Joy Through the Gospel of Luke: A Christmas to Calvary Advent Countdown* (Enumclaw, WA: Redemption Press, 2021).

66. Ruth Chou Simons, *Fields of Joy* (Eugene, OR: Harvest House, 2020).

67. Ruth Chou Simons, *Fields of Joy* (Eugene, OR: Harvest House, 2020), 19.

68. Ruth Chou Simons, *Fields of Joy* (Eugene, OR: Harvest House, 2020), 5.

69. Robert Jamieson, A.R. Fausset, & David Brown, *Commentary Critical and Explanatory on the Whole Bible,* Vol. 2 (1871; Bellingham, WA: Faithlife, 1997), 368.

70. Charles F. Stanley, *Charles F. Stanley's Handbook for Christian Living: Biblical Answers to Life's Tough Questions* (Nashville, TN: Thomas Nelson, 2008), 193.

71. David Jeremiah, *Searching for Heaven on Earth Journal: How to Find What Really Matters in Life* (Nashville, TN: Thomas Nelson, 2007), 82.

72. John Eldredge, *Resilient: Restoring Your Weary Soul in These Turbulent Times* (Nashville, TN: Thomas Nelson, 2022), 7.

73. Cynthia Cavanaugh, *Anchored: Leading through the Storms* (Birmingham, AL: New Hope, 2018), 167.

74. Kay Arthur, *As Silver Refined: Learning to Embrace Life's Disappointments* (Colorado Springs: Waterbrook, 2009), 117.

75. Johann Peter Lange, Philip Schaff, G. F .C. Fronmüller, & J. Isidor Mombert, *A Commentary on the Holy Scriptures: 1 Peter* (Bellingham, WA: Faithlife, 2008), 91.

ORDER INFORMATION

To order additional copies of this book, please visit
www.redemption-press.com.
Also available at Christian bookstores, Amazon, and Barnes and Noble.

Printed in the USA
CPSIA information can be obtained
at www.ICGtesting.com
LVHW061259290823
756621LV00011B/329